Here's why you should read this book: Dr. Iris Delgado writes with clarity. Though highly educated, she writes in a style that any reader can understand. When you read what she writes, you'll get it! Iris writes from experience rather than theory. She has experienced what she is writing about. Her children and her grandchildren are living examples of people whose hearts have been perfected through the power of prayer. Iris Delgado is a prayer warrior! She holds the powers of darkness at bay through relentlessly placing her petitions before God's throne. You will not regret taking the time to read and absorb this powerful narrative on prayer!

—J. Don George
Founding Pastor, Calvary Church, Irving, Texas

Iris Delgado has written many powerful, impacting books, but this one is really tops. She has captured the power of older leaders in the family releasing blessing over all the children—from earliest age. This practice of prayers of protection and blessing is a tradition that every Christian home should adopt. This is a must-have, must-do book that will change you and your family—forever.

—Apostle Naomi Dowdy
Naomi Dowdy Ministries, Singapore

I have been married to Iris for forty-eight wonderful years, and I can honestly say that she is truly a woman of God. The Lord uses her effectively and powerfully to minister to women and families throughout the United States and abroad. Her example and her prayers have anchored my family and produced a loving and unbreakable bond among my daughters and grandchildren. I highly recommend this prayer book to every parent, no matter what age your children may be or what situation they may find themselves in today. I recommend that you not only read this book but also put it into practice.

—John Delgado
President, Texas University of Theology, Euless, Texas

My mother, Iris Delgado, has been an incredible example of a praying mother. From my childhood to my own parenthood, I have seen with my own eyes the power that prayer can have in any situation. We live in a day that our children are under outside influences from every direction of their lives. Social media and cell phones have opened a whole new level of intensity of influence that we never experienced in our youth. We will never be able to remove all the bad, but we can call on heaven to help guard our children as they are exposed to so many things beyond our control. This new book gives practical tools and advice, along with prayers, to teach you how to pray effectively. Whether you are new to praying for your children or have calloused knees from years of warfare, this book will be a worthy investment to your family and the generations that will follow you, covered under the shelter of the Almighty.

—KATHY DELGADO-CHATTERTON
AUTHOR, DON'T BE SCARED TO TELL
WWW.FACEBOOK.COM/DONTBESCAREDTOTELL
DONTBESCAREDTOTELL.COM
EULESS, TEXAS

POWERFUL
PRAYERS
to Protect

the of

YOUR
CHILD

POWERFUL PRAYERS to Protect

the *of*

YOUR CHILD

IRIS DELGADO

CHARISMA
HOUSE

Most CHARISMA HOUSE BOOK GROUP products are available at special quantity discounts for bulk purchase for sales promotions, premiums, fundraising, and educational needs. For details, write Charisma House Book Group, 600 Rinehart Road, Lake Mary, Florida 32746, or telephone (407) 333-0600.

POWERFUL PRAYERS TO PROTECT THE HEART OF YOUR CHILD
by Iris Delgado
Published by Charisma House
Charisma Media/Charisma House Book Group
600 Rinehart Road
Lake Mary, Florida 32746
www.charismahouse.com

Unless otherwise noted, all Scripture quotations are taken from the New King James Version®. Copyright © 1982 by Thomas Nelson. Used by permission. All rights reserved.

Scripture quotations marked AMP are from the Amplified Bible. Copyright © 2015 by The Lockman Foundation. Used by permission. www.Lockman.org

Scripture quotations marked AMPC are from the Amplified Bible, Classic Edition. Copyright © 1954, 1958, 1962, 1964, 1965, 1987 by The Lockman Foundation. Used by permission. www.Lockman.org

Scripture quotations marked ESV are from the Holy Bible, English Standard Version. Copyright © 2001 by Crossway Bibles, a division of Good News Publishers. Used by permission.

Scripture quotations marked ISV are from the International Standard Version. Copyright © 1995–2014 by ISV Foundation. All rights reserved internationally. Used by permission of Davidson Press, LLC.

Scripture quotations marked MSG are from The Message: The Bible in Contemporary English, copyright © 1993, 1994, 1995, 1996, 2000, 2001, 2002. Used by permission of NavPress Publishing Group.

Visit the author's website at www.crownedwithpurpose.com or irisdelgadobooks.com.

Library of Congress Cataloging-in-Publication Data:
An application to register this book for cataloging has been submitted to the Library of Congress.
International Standard Book Number: 978-1-62999-612-7
E-book ISBN: 978-1-62999-613-4

This publication is translated in Spanish under the title *Oraciones poderosas para proteger el corazón de tus hijos*, copyright © 2019 by Iris Delgado, published by Casa Creación, a Charisma Media company. All rights reserved.

Portions of this book's content were previously published in *Satan, You Can't Have My Children*, Charisma House, 2011, and *Satan, You Can't Have My Promises*, Charisma House, 2013.

19 20 21 22 23 — 9 8 7 6 5 4 3 2 1
Printed in the United States of America

I dedicate this labor of love and earnest importance to my two daughters, Kristine and Kathy; to my two grandsons, Daniel and Gabriel; and to all the children who will be the recipients of these powerful and effective prayers.

These focused and specific prayers, full of the Word of God, have delivered our daughters and grandchildren from the enemy's camp and have caused a very intimate and unbreakable friendship among our family.

I stand in the gap with all the parents who will make a positive decision to make these specific and powerful prayers for their children. I have no doubt that you will also see great miracles and radical changes in the lives of your loved ones. To God be all the glory!

CONTENTS

INTRODUCTION

*Prayer does not equip us for greater
works—prayer is the greater work.*
—OSWALD CHAMBERS

HAVE YOU NOTICED that this generation is greatly
wounded and many young people have no direction in
life? Many of them have grown up without a father or
mother. A generation of children with orphan hearts is seeking
meaning and acceptance in all the wrong places. But I believe a
great awakening is taking place right now, and we will see many of
our wayward children and young people come back to God.

I consider the assignment of writing this book to be even more
critical and of urgent need than all the other books that God has
given me the privilege of writing. It is imperative that we decide to
impact the lives of our children and grandchildren for generations
to come by covering them with powerful and dynamic prayers that
will protect their hearts.

There are many homes in crisis today, battling the problems
of the children. We are looking at a generation fascinated by the
magic of every new technology and social network that absorbs
and captivates all their attention and their senses. We are also witnessing tremendous social changes that are profoundly impressing
this generation, causing many family problems as well as difficulties in children's studies. Sadly there is an alarming rise in the

number of suicides, not only among adults but also among our children and youth.

According to experts and counselors, within fifteen years we may see an entire generation with memory deprivation, processing difficulties, poor grammar, attention deficits, and digital addictions. It will also be known as a generation that prefers risk over calculated and well-thought-out decisions.

WHY THIS BOOK MATTERS

Why do I have so much faith that prayers such as the ones I've included in this book can and will protect, redeem, and save your child from the clutches of the enemy? I have this unwavering confidence in my heart because, although I experienced humiliation, rejection, and abuse as a child, I had the great blessing of having a mother and grandmother who prayed powerful and explosive prayers and declarations of faith that rose up to heaven like a cyclone. Their prayers are the reason I am able to write this book and I'm not stuck in a life of misery and hopelessness.

The simplicity of these powerful prayers and declarations of faith will help you practice a dynamic spiritual exercise that will surpass your understanding and reach the root of every adverse situation. Prayer is the means by which we spiritually connect with the Creator of heaven and earth, our heavenly Father. Prayer is the gasoline that fires up the motor and takes it to its destination. Powerful prayers filled with the Word of God, prayed by a man or woman who believes God, are very effective to protect the lives and souls of our loved ones and to break strongholds and all demonic assignments.

It took me many years, since the time my daughters were very young, to compose and write in my diary many of these scriptures, declarations, and lessons about powerful and effective prayer. I have also had the great honor of sharing these prayers and teachings with mothers and fathers in churches and at conferences around the world, and I have received many messages and emails testifying about the positive results in the lives of their children and family members.

My daughters and my grandsons are the joy and crown of my life. These powerful prayers have been part of their spiritual growth and have also served as a hedge of protection and spiritual covering from demonic attacks in their daily walk. No weapon formed against them can prosper or have an adverse effect. I firmly believe what God has promised in His Word, and I will continue to deposit powerful prayers into their lives every day, no matter how old they are.

No other exercise is more powerful than your fervent prayers to rescue your children from the evil wave that is submerging them. No worrying, anxiety, tears of desperation, or even counseling can have the effect that powerful prayers in the mouth of a tenacious parent will have in tearing down spiritual strongholds and freeing a son or daughter from darkness, corruption, and eternal damnation.

This book has been organized into two parts. The first part prepares you as the parent. It contains teaching and prayers that will help you understand that you are in a spiritual battle and what your spiritual weapons are. It will help you prepare your own heart and mind before you pray so that your prayers will be as effective as possible.

The second part of this book contains prayers and declarations you can begin praying over your child of any age and in any situation. Determine today to read the contents of this book, and do not neglect the opportunity to make these prayers and declarations part of your daily life. Powerful prayers and declarations filled with the Word of God are the spiritual lifeguards that will save your child!

I highly recommend that you make a habit of praying some of these prayers every day. They are intended to be examples of how you can pray based on my own experiences of praying for my children and grandchildren. As your prayer life grows, I believe the Lord will give you additional scriptures to declare over your children and prayers to pray for them at every age and in every situation they face in life. That's why I've provided room for you to write additional scriptures and prayers for your child at the end of each chapter as you follow the Holy Spirit's leading.

Highlight and mark the prayers most needed, and carry this book everywhere you go. Pray with authority! Your prayers will be seeds planted in the hearts of your children and grandchildren, no matter what age they are. Even if it takes a while, expect to see results and a harvest of good fruit.

The Word of God is alive, active, and powerful! It is the most significant force against the kingdom of darkness. Your child belongs to God and not to the devil! Pray for your child effectively and powerfully!

Prayer for Strength and Perseverance

I have prayed for everyone who reads this book. As I write this introduction, I want to include my prayer that you will not waver or lose heart as you seek to pray faithfully for your child throughout his or her life.

> *Dear Father God, I lift in prayer every person who has decided to enter this journey of actively praying for his or her children and loved ones. Give these people the strength and tenacity to remain committed and faithful in this important and urgent task.*
>
> *Open their spiritual eyes to understand the warfare they face for the hearts of their children and families. Activate them with courage and boldness to defend their territory and claim the promises that have already been prepared for them.*
>
> *Unleash a fresh anointing of prayer upon them so they can declare Your Word and powerful prayers over their loved ones. "For the weapons of our warfare are not*

carnal but mighty in God for pulling down strongholds" (2 Cor. 10:4). *In the name of Jesus, amen.*

Here's a prayer you can add to mine and pray over yourself as you begin this journey:

Thank You, Father, for Your great love, protection, and provision. Thank You for saving us from all of the evil strategies and plans of the enemy. I rest in Your care as I prepare to pray for my children. In the name of Jesus, amen.

THE MIRACLES ARE IN YOU!

As I conclude this introduction, I want to challenge you to speak the Word. The Word creates miracles and does the impossible. You must act! You can't remain passive. As I will explain in the opening chapters of this book, you are in spiritual warfare for the souls of your family, especially your children.

The good news is that God is holy and faithful to His word. Don't be afraid to pray powerfully the words of the Scriptures, casting out all fears. Bring every thought captive to the obedience of Christ.

Are you ready to get started? Then in the name of Jesus cast out the lies of the enemy, and declare, "My family belongs to the kingdom of God!"

PART I

PREPARE YOURSELF

*Those things which proceed out of
the mouth come from the heart.*
—MATTHEW 15:18

Chapter 1

BEFORE YOU BEGIN

*Now this is the confidence that we have in Him, that if
we ask anything according to His will, He hears us. And
if we know that He hears us, whatever we ask, we know
that we have the petitions that we have asked of Him.*
—1 JOHN 5:14–15

YOUR PRAYERS ARE a powerful tool to protect and transform
your child's heart throughout his or her life. As you pray
the prayers and declarations of faith provided in this book,
believe in your heart that God hears your prayers and the Word of
God never returns empty. This will have a significant effect in the
spiritual realm and also in the natural world.

Some of you will be praying for your babies, toddlers, or young
children, others have preadolescent children or teens, and still
others have adult children. Your children may be married or even
parents themselves. (You can pray for your son- or daughter-in-
law too.) Your child may be a foster child, an adopted child, or a
stepchild. Some of you will be praying for grandchildren, extended
family members, or children you teach or take care of.

It is possible that you are praying for a child who has strayed
from the ways of God and is roaming aimlessly through the world
with the wrong friends. The situation in your family might be
complicated, challenging, and even devastating. Crisis and chaos

in a home are signs that the enemy, Satan, is working full time to destroy the family. Where chaos and confusion abound, there are malignant spirits at work.

I advise you to submit to God in repentance and ask for His help. He is greater than the enemy, and He can heal and restore lives. I pray that the prayers, teaching, and encouragement you find in this book will act as a healing balm from God that renews your faith and hope.

Powerful Prayers

It is essential to understand that these prayers are provided as examples of how you can pray prayers supported by the Word of God, which is alive and active. There's nothing wrong with praying the words that have been provided. In fact, I encourage you to keep this book with you at all times so you can refer to it as needed. But you can also pray using your own words as the Holy Spirit leads you. Either way, it is important not to allow your thoughts to be diverted while you are praying for your children. Learn to focus your mind and heart, and believe that every prayer that comes out of your mouth is like a warring sword, defeating all the enemy's plans against your children, your grandchildren, and your family.

Pray fervently and with passion to invade and destroy the darkness in the life of a loved one. Pray for wisdom to make right decisions. Pray that God will enlarge your tent (your sphere of influence and everything that concerns you). Pray to break the bondage of poverty. Pray to release yourself from curses and negative family attachments. Your powerful prayers will break yokes (bad habits, oppression, sickness, demonic mental attacks, depression, burdens, bondage, repression, addictions, and every work of the enemy)!

DECLARATIONS OF FAITH

In addition to sample prayers, I provide you with many powerful declarations that are based on the Scriptures. This is merely another way to pray for your child and to use the Word of God, which is the sword of the Spirit, to do spiritual battle against the enemy.

Declare and prophesy (predict with God-given authority) powerful Scripture-based statements such as those I have written in this book. The Holy Spirit may direct you to other scriptures you can speak out loud as declarations over your specific situation or need. Pray them with boldness for your child or loved one.

ARM YOURSELF FOR SPIRITUAL BATTLE

It is critical to understand that we are in a spiritual war. Genuine faith in the heart of a believer has the power to change outward circumstances to a desired outcome.

"For though we live in the world, we do not wage war as the world does. The weapons we fight with are not the weapons of the world. On the contrary, they have divine power to demolish strongholds" (2 Cor. 10:3–4, NIV). Your faith in God's Word and your powerful prayers will be the key for overcoming the powers of the enemy against you and your family.

It would be unwise to engage in an actual war without armor or weapons. The same is true about waging spiritual warfare successfully. You must be willing as a parent to continually submit yourself to God and to continually resist the devil. James 4:7 is very specific: "Submit yourselves, then, to God. Resist the devil, and he will flee from you" (NIV).

When a parent is truly submitted to God and resisting the devil, then the devil must flee! Yes, the devil has no choice but to flee from a Christian parent who is truly and totally submitted to almighty God. This is spiritual warfare!

Learn how to use and rely on the following powerful weapons of spiritual warfare. In my book *Satan, You Can't Have My Children,* in chapter 1, "Spiritual Warfare to Save Our Children," you will find very good advice about this spiritual war we are all involved in and how we resist the devil by using the proper weapons God has already provided for us. God has guaranteed the victory through:

The name of Jesus—Make all your prayers in the name of Jesus (Eph. 5:20; Phil. 2:10).

The power of the blood of Jesus—As a believer, you can overcome Satan's attacks on yourself and your children by the blood of the Lamb (Jesus Christ) and by the word of your testimony (Rev. 12:11). Every time you pray and declare God's Word in faith, you are testifying. The blood of Jesus also has the power to cleanse you of all your sins (1 John 1:7). Sin has always separated man from God. The blood covenant has given man a way out from eternal condemnation. There's power in the blood of Jesus. Learn to pray specifically (adding the names): *I apply the blood of Jesus over my child, spouse, home, and mind. Thank You, Father God, for cleansing us from all sin and redeeming us from the hand of the enemy. In Jesus' name, amen.*

The power of the Holy Spirit—Depend entirely on His help, teaching, and friendship. Don't be afraid to pray in the language of the Holy Spirit every day (Jude 20). Praying in other tongues is very effective and powerful. He will be the best personal friend you will ever have. Learn not to ignore Him by communicating with Him every day. He will also help you pray when you don't know what to pray (Rom. 8:26–27).

Also, the Bible says that you will "receive power (ability, efficiency, and might) when the Holy Spirit has come upon you" (Acts 1:8, AMPC). He is always waiting to help and guide. Some of the attributes of the Holy Spirit are listed here (AMPC):

+ Teacher (Luke 12:12; 1 John 2:27)

+ Helper (John 15:26)

+ Guide (John 16:13)

+ Comforter (John 14:26; 15:26)

+ Counselor (John 14:26; 15:26)

+ Intercessor (John 14:26: 15:26)

+ Advocate (John 14:26; 15:26)

+ Strengthener (John 14:26; 15:26)

+ Standby (John 14:26; 15:26)

The power of praise and worship—Worship and praise with hymns, songs, psalms, and prayers of thankfulness. Praise can be verbalized and expressed through singing, lifting your hands, clapping, and giving adoration to God for who He is and His names (Ps. 47:1; 63:4). Worship is demonstrated by our prayer of reverence and awe, surrender of our entire being, and expression of adoration and thanksgiving to our Creator and God Almighty. This kind of prayer is more important and effective than all other prayers we make. The enemy hates praise and worship. Feel free to just relax in God's presence as you "worship the Father in the Spirit and in truth" (John 4:23–24, NIV).

The effective prayer—Do not memorize prayers (including the prayers in this book) or use prayers asking only for needs. Effective prayer is dynamic, original, specific, and according to the Word of God.

Learn to cleanse yourself by renouncing all sins and unforgiveness. Your effective prayers for cleansing will release healing and transformation and will "renew a steadfast spirit" in you (Ps. 51:10). Learn to pray with fervency, always thanking God for the answers to your requests and wisdom and understanding to pray with the guidance of the Holy Spirit (John 16:13; Jas. 5:16).

The Word of God—Declare portions of the Word, such as Psalm 91 and God's promises. The Word of God is alive, active, and powerful and blesses the believer who obeys it (Heb. 4:12; 11:28; Ps. 107:20). Make time each day to meditate on a portion of the Word, asking the Holy Spirit to help you understand it (Josh. 1:8).

The prayer of agreement—This prayer is very effective when we agree with another believer, joining together in one mind in faith. Find a prayer partner in your church or prayer group who will agree to pray together with you concerning your specific request and believe that God will answer your petition (Matt. 18:19). Don't be afraid to be bold and specific. If you're standing for the salvation and healing of a son or daughter, believe that God will answer and bring restoration, no matter how long it takes.

As you arm yourself to enter into this spiritual battle, declare and believe the following powerful statements of faith:

In the name of Jesus I resist the enemy, and he must flee from me. I surrender to the control of Jesus Christ as my Lord and Savior (Jas. 4:7).

I claim my union as an heir of God through Christ Jesus (Gal. 4:7).

In the name of Jesus I bind all the works of the enemy and forbid him to interfere in my life and in my family (Matt. 18:18).

I claim the blood of Jesus over my family and declare that God has given me authority over all the power of the enemy and nothing will hurt my family or me (Luke 9:1; 10:19).

In the name of Jesus I bring every thought captive to the obedience of Christ. I come against all lies of the enemy, and I set my mind on those things that are pure, lovely, and praiseworthy (2 Cor. 10:5; Phil. 4:8).

My lips will praise and worship almighty God because He is faithful (Ps. 89:8).

THE HOLY SPIRIT'S HELP

As I mentioned in the list of spiritual warfare weapons, we must depend on the help of the Holy Spirit when we pray. We must learn to talk with Him and ask Him for direction. Ask Him to open the right doors and close the wrong ones. Ask Him to teach you how to pray correctly and with boldness.

For the Holy Spirit will teach you in that very hour what you ought to say.
—LUKE 12:12

Or do you not know that your body is the temple of the Holy Spirit who is in you, whom you have from God, and you are not your own?
—1 CORINTHIANS 6:19

> But you, beloved, building yourselves up on your most
> holy faith, praying in the Holy Spirit.
>
> —JUDE 20

When we have needs in life, whom do we look for? We seek our Father God because He is the giver of all good and perfect gifts. The fountain is the Father. But the giver of that fountain is Christ, and the power of the fountain is the Holy Spirit.

The Holy Spirit is your helper. He is your assistant, helping you receive everything that pertains to life and holiness and everything that God has already provided for you.

> And I will pray the Father, and He will give you
> another Helper, that He may abide with you forever—
> the Spirit of truth, whom the world cannot receive,
> because it neither sees Him nor knows Him; but you
> know Him, for He dwells with you and will be in you.
>
> —JOHN 14:16–17

Here's a prayer to ask for the Holy Spirit's help as you begin this journey of praying for the hearts of your children:

> *Dear Lord, as I pray for my children, I ask for Your Holy Spirit to work in their hearts and teach them to connect with You in all their decisions. Lord, my children need to have a personal encounter with You so that their lives can be transformed and they can touch others with Your love and Your presence.*
>
> *Holy Spirit, help them to know You personally so that they always come to You for help, teaching, and friendship. Cause them to know You as their Guide, Teacher, Friend, Comforter, and Advocate. In the name of the Father, Son, and Holy Spirit, amen!*

KEY POINTS TO REMEMBER

Following are some key points to keep in mind as you pray for your child or loved one. I've learned these things over the years of praying for my own children and grandchildren, and these things are essential to remember as you pray.

1. Don't limit God.

Don't put God in a box. Don't ask Him for small things. Ask for all His promises. Nothing is impossible for Him. Never underestimate God and all His precious promises to His children.

2. Be obedient to God's Word.

The Holy Spirit is always watching and listening attentively to see how He can help you and respond to your needs. But He is motivated and challenged only by God's Word and your obedience. The moment you declare God's Word, as you walk in obedience, the Holy Spirit acts upon His Word to perform it!

3. Do not stay passive.

Fill your heart with good things, and out of your mouth will come good things, good words, sound counsel, and good ideas. What you put in will come out. Read the Bible every day, and ask the Holy Spirit for understanding.

4. What you sow, you will reap.

You will never have abundance unless you are sowing all the time! The more you give, the more you will have. If you have little, check your giving habits. Sow into good ground. Give to the poor, to missions, to the needy. Give your tithe to the storehouse (where you get fed spiritually). Start with the little you may have, and keep increasing it. It's a spiritual law—the law of sowing and reaping. Like the law of gravity, when it is set into motion, there is no stopping it.

5. Stop being a victim.

If you have been hurt by someone and are still carrying the pain, hurt, and shame, it is time to put a stop to it. As long as you insist on dwelling and remembering all the feelings of the pain of abuse, hurt, divorce, trauma, negative words, barrenness, an unkind parent, and so on, you will never feel peace and victory in your life. You must release that thing—it is like a cancer that keeps eating away at you. I'll discuss this more in the next chapter.

6. Forgive the person or people who hurt you.

Release yourself and break the curse of bondage over your life. Set into action God's blessings! Loose yourself today! I was there years ago, but today I am free. It took a specific decision on my part. Once I said, "I forgive you, Dad," I was free. The chains came off. I understand your pain, but if you want to move forward, you must stop feeling sorry for yourself and get over it! The best of your life is ahead of you. Your children and your children's children will inherit your freedom and God's promises and not the curses of abuse and lack. In the next chapter I'll explain more about this and provide you with powerful prayers to help you forgive.

7. Pray with intention and not passively or ritually.

Prayer is a common practice among the majority of Christians. It can become a habit to recite the same quick prayers all the time instead of prayers that are full of life because they are specific and focused and able to tear down strongholds in our lives and the life of the child or person we are praying for.

Many times our prayers look like a to-do list that we make for shopping or running errands. To avoid this, we have to examine what we are praying. Let's begin by asking some questions. I've left room for you to write your answers.

Are my prayers effective?

_____

_____

_____

Is God answering my prayers, or does it seem He does not hear me?

_____

_____

_____

Whom am I praying for? Am I concentrating my petitions on myself?

_____

_____

_____

What am I asking the Lord to do?

_____

_____

_____

_____

Have I looked attentively in the Word for wisdom, or do I just wish that God would intervene in my plans and problems?

_____

_____

_____

Am I praying only during emergencies?

_____

_____

_____

The majority of us struggle to enter into the presence of God and surrender ourselves until God touches our hearts with a new perspective and hope. It is important we learn to fill our hearts with Scriptures that will sustain us and help us to pray powerfully.

Our lives will be more effective as individuals, parents, and spouses if we align our petitions with the will and the Word of God and believe in faith that He will do what He says He will do (Mark 11:24). Then we can pray with certainty and confidence, knowing that He hears us and will answer our petitions.

GET TO THE HEART

Use this space to write down the names of people you will be praying for and any prayers or Scripture verses that the Lord is bringing to your mind as you prepare to pray.

Chapter 2

PREPARE YOUR HEART TO PRAY

The effective, fervent prayer of a righteous man avails much.
—JAMES 5:16

A S YOU KNOW by now, this book provides you with examples of powerful prayers and declarations of faith that will have a tremendous impact on your heart and the heart of your child. No matter what your specific situation or need to stand in the gap for your child, God is attentive to your prayers. They have the power to carry out what the Word of God declares. God's promises are for all His children. Pray with boldness and fervency.

Before you pray for others, it is important to examine your own heart and make sure it is right with God. See if there is any fear, frustration, unforgiveness, anguish, or condemnation for things that are happening or have happened in your family. Ask Him to forgive you of all your sins and offenses and everything that you know does not please Him. Forgive those who have hurt or offended you, and ask the Holy Spirit to help you overcome the offenses and abuse.

I remember when I was in my own prison of hate and unforgiveness. I hated my father so much I wished him dead every day. For many years after the child abuse I experienced, I imagined him dead in a car accident. Forgiving him was totally out of the question. A few years after I was married, I received valuable teaching about soul healing and transformation. I learned that hate is a stronghold that would keep me in prison as long as I allowed it. I also learned that if I allowed God to heal my heart, I would have the capacity to forgive my father. I realized I was a prisoner, and I desired to really be free. When I finally surrendered my life and my burdens to God, and I said a prayer asking God to forgive my father and forgive me for hating him, I experienced a deep release and a sense of well-being. I came out of prison! From then on I was different. The transformation healed my emotions and opened doors of blessing, not only for me but also for my household.

This step is crucial. You can't go by feelings here. If you need help, here is a sample prayer to say with all your heart:

> *Lord Jesus, I bring to memory before You [name of the person/people you need to forgive]. I feel hurt and offended by this person/these people, and I confess the negative feelings I have toward him/her/them.*
>
> *I am ready to forgive all the harm they did to me, and at this moment I forgive them for the pain and hatred they caused me. I release them and surrender them to You! Thank You, my Lord, for this deliverance. Help me to live without resentment and bitterness. Fill me with Your joy and Your love. In the name of Jesus, amen!*

Continue this prayer by saying:

> *I bind all anxiety, worry, stress, doubt, unbelief, impatience, and fear. I release God's peace, love, strength, wisdom, knowledge, and understanding into my life. I declare that I have a sound mind and that my body is the temple of the Holy Spirit.*

Now enter into God's presence with thanksgiving. Thank Him for all His blessings. Here's an example of what to say:

Dear God, I belong to You. I thank You, Father, for this privilege. I declare that You are the only and true living God. Today I reverence You and acknowledge that without You I cannot survive. I need You.

I believe that the power that raised Christ from the dead lives in me and has set me free from darkness, sin, iniquity, death, and all disease. I declare that the blood of Jesus cleanses me and protects me. I apply the blood of Jesus to my thoughts, my heart, my body, and my family as I prepare to enter into prayer for my loved ones.

Help me, Holy Spirit, to pray fearlessly and with boldness. I acknowledge You as my spiritual Guide and my Helper. Thank You for filling my heart and my mind with these powerful prayers and helping me to understand the tactics of the enemy and how to overcome in this spiritual warfare.

Conclude this sample prayer by relinquishing all burdens and preparing your heart to make prayers and powerful declarations for the salvation, health, and well-being of your child.

Dear Father, I submit to You at this moment, believing in the truth of Your Word and the authority that we have over all the power of the enemy (Luke 10:19). I cast out all fear and condemnation.

I choose to be grateful, to rest in You, to let go of my worries about my child, to trust You, and to give up all my burdens. I realize that living in doubt can stop the flow of Your blessings. Your Word declares in Proverbs 15:8 that the prayers of the upright are Your delight.

I surrender to You, Father, and I ask You to forgive me of all my sins and offenses. Help me to serve You with all my heart and to be an example of Your love and kindness in my home. Thank You, Holy Spirit, for guiding my

*prayers and helping me know the workings of the enemy.
In the name of Jesus, amen.*

DON'T FORGET ABOUT YOUR EMOTIONS

As a Christian parent, you need to live a life that represents God. Your character must be strong and steadfast in Christ if you want to be a dynamic example of God's love for your children. If you've just prayed a prayer to forgive someone, your emotions may need time to catch up. That's understandable, but whether or not your heart is healing during the process of forgiveness, you need to keep your emotions under control.

I remember when I allowed my circumstances to control my emotions. I would spend the day depressed and miserable. But I learned that God has created us with the ability to change. We can control ourselves with the help of the Holy Spirit and the cleansing of the Word of God. We have to believe it!

The first thing we must do is stop making excuses. What is an excuse? It is a pretext, an apology; it is to self-justify, to decline, to be defensive; it is to give up, to fall back or fall away. We have the power of God in us that enables us to stop making excuses for our bad behavior or bad choices and to exercise self-control.

As children of the kingdom of God, we are capable and have wisdom and understanding. We are in the army of God Almighty. We have backup. We have a guide and a bodyguard. We are automatically enrolled at the university of the kingdom of God, and discipleship is our lifelong training course.

We have to learn to be faithful in attending the discipleship of the kingdom every day. We can't be absent or make excuses. The Holy Spirit is the teacher, always hoping that we get to class. When we pray and open the Bible, immediately class begins.

God is ready to put His Word to work in your life and in your home. "Then the LORD said to me, 'You have seen well, for I am ready to perform My word'" (Jer. 1:12). It is important that you learn to depend on and rest in His Spirit and His strength to do the things you need to do. It is the only way you will be able to handle your emotions and your decisions.

Don't forget that we are in a spiritual war. The enemy, Satan, comes against the children of God in many ways, but those who win this war are steadfast in Christ Jesus.

Philippians 1:28 tells us not to be afraid of our enemies. It says if we behave with courage, we will see them destroyed and we will be saved because God will give us the victory. This scripture tells us that God and the devil are watching us. When there is a difficult situation, we have to choose how to act. Either we remain in peace, or we allow our emotions to take control of us. Here is where our level of trust and faith in God is demonstrated.

It doesn't matter how much we say we trust God; if we are always depressed, combative, and negative, our trust is not in God. God wants us to learn to trust and depend on Him through the good and the bad times.

Being a Christian does not mean we will never have problems; it means that when the challenges and fear come, God gives us grace to pass through the fire and the storms and exit on the other side without even the smell of smoke (Dan. 3:27).

> And Moses said to the people, "Do not be afraid. Stand still, and see the salvation of the LORD, which He will accomplish for you today. For the Egyptians whom you see today, you shall see again no more forever. The LORD will fight for you, and you shall hold your peace."
>
> —EXODUS 14:13–14

Remember that God is always with you and He fights for you. When He allows difficult situations, you can trust that He is in control, and in the end you will see His glory shine upon your family.

DECLARATIONS OF FAITH

Before I conclude this chapter, I want to give you some declarations of faith that will help to prepare your heart to pray for your child. As you speak these scriptures, decree that your request is completed in the name of Jesus!

Even though my own body is under attack by an incurable disease, I stand firm each day, making these declarations, and I see God's mighty hand sustain me. I keep going and doing, and it never stops me from achieving my goals. Make these promises yours! Believe God and His Word!

> Father God, today I set into action Your covenant promises. I declare that no weapon formed against my family or me will prosper (Isa. 54:17).
>
> No evil, sickness, accidents, interruptions, lack, poverty, robberies, fear, sudden death, pestilence, mind attacks, lies, temptations, or insatiable desires (ravenous, unappeasable cravings, addictive desires) will come near my dwelling (body), or affect my life or my loved ones. Ezekiel 37:27 (NIV) says, "My dwelling place will be with them; I will be their God, and they will be my people." (See also Psalm 91 and Isaiah 32:18.)
>
> I am the righteousness of God in Christ Jesus (2 Cor. 5:21).
>
> I declare that greater is Christ in me than the enemy who is in this world (1 John 4:4).
>
> I believe You are guiding and instructing my loved ones and me in all our ways (John 16:13; Ps. 37:23).

My spouse is growing in the grace and knowledge of Jesus Christ, and he/she is full of wisdom, knowledge, and understanding to be all that You have created him/her to be (2 Pet. 3:18; Col. 1:9; Prov. 9:10). (You can say this for your future wife/husband if you are single. Speak it by faith into existence.)

The Word of God is a lamp that shines on my feet and a light that illuminates every step I take (Prov. 6:23; Ps. 27:1).

I walk in Your fullness, guided by the Holy Spirit and hedged around and about by the protection of Your angelic hosts (Ps. 34:7; 91:9–11; 121:8).

I have the mind of Christ, and today I will make wise decisions and prosperous investments (1 Cor. 2:16; Ps. 115:14; Zech. 8:12).

Thank You, my Lord, for supplying everything I need today (Phil. 4:19).

Thank You, Holy Spirit, for directing my life and teaching me truth (Ps. 25:5).

Thank You, God, for keeping me from all temptation and procrastination, laziness, putting things off, and unfinished business (Jas. 1:12–15; Prov. 19:15). I give You all the glory. In Christ's name, amen!

GET TO THE HEART

Use this space to write down the names of people you have chosen to forgive or other ways the Lord has helped you to prepare your heart, along with any prayers or Scripture verses the Lord is bringing to mind.

_____

_____

_____

_____

_____

_____

_____

_____

_____

_____

_____

_____

_____

_____

_____

_____

_____

_____

_____

Chapter 3

PREPARE YOUR MIND TO PRAY

For as he thinks in his heart, so is he.
—**Proverbs 23:7**

O NE OF THE most important things that I recently have learned to do with more skill is *choose on purpose* what I think or even allow to enter my thoughts. This revelation of the Holy Spirit has taken me out of a bed of sickness, which the enemy hoped I would never get up from, to continue giving powerful teachings and counsel. I believe this fresh insight and the powerful, targeted prayers that accompany it will positively affect your life as well as your children and grandchildren.

Our thoughts can be measured, they can be positive or negative, and they affect every area of our lives. They influence every decision we make, every word we say, every action we take, and every reaction we have.

If we want our prayers to be effective in tearing down strongholds and protecting the lives of our children and grandchildren, we must first learn to renew our minds with the Word of God. There can be no doubt or confusion. If we allow doubt, stress, and adverse circumstances that many times surround our families to take control of our thoughts, we will never be able to pray freely or be confident that God is attentive to our prayers and that soon we will see the victory.

It is urgent that we understand this teaching. If we do not learn how to bring every thought captive to the obedience of Christ (2 Cor. 10:5), we will never live the overcoming life that Jesus Christ died to provide for us—a life of peace and joy and a happy home with well-adjusted children and the sustenance of all we need. We must choose what the Word of truth says more than what our feelings or our difficulties dictate.

The next section of this chapter will list many specific scriptures about the mind. I prefer that you study these scriptures well because they are much more important than my own words. One way to comply with these instructions is to take a little time every day to think carefully about a promise in the Bible that can renew your mind and then make a short and spontaneous prayer, entering into agreement with the Word of God. My book *Satan, You Can't Have My Promises* is full of wonderful promises you can believe and appropriate for your spiritual growth. Don't forget to thank the Holy Spirit for helping you and directing your steps and thoughts.

This daily regimen will help you to focus more specifically your prayers for yourself and your children. This is a regimen I personally practice every day, and it has given me wonderful results. All my family members serve God, and they are full of blessings and provision. I can personally attest to the fact that praying according to the Word of God is powerful and effective.

KEY VERSES ABOUT THE MIND

Let's take a look at Romans 12:2 in three different Bible translations, which are all worded differently but mean the same thing.

> Do not be conformed to this world, but be transformed by the renewal of your mind, that by testing you may discern what is the will of God, what is good and acceptable and perfect.
> —ROMANS 12:2, ESV

23

Do not conform to the pattern of this world, but be transformed by the renewing of your mind. Then you will be able to test and approve what God's will is—his good, pleasing and perfect will.

—Romans 12:2, niv

Don't copy the behavior and customs of this world, but let God transform you into a new person by changing the way you think. Then you will learn to know God's will for you, which is good and pleasing and perfect.

—Romans 12:2, nlt

The Holy Spirit wants to teach us how to discern God's will and how to change. It is the Holy Spirit who wants to help us change the way we think and how we process our thoughts. *Discern* means "to see, recognize, or understand something."[1] *Change* means "to make different; to replace."[2]

As you begin this process, take time to study these powerful scriptures, which I've organized into topics for you.

Promises of a renewed mind

+ Titus 3:5—You are saved and regenerated through the Holy Spirit operating in your mind.

+ Psalm 51:10—When you sincerely repent, your spirit is entirely renewed.

+ 2 Corinthians 4:16—Every day your "inward man" (your mind) is being renewed as you apply the Word of God.

+ 1 Corinthians 2:16—You have "the mind of Christ."

Meditation renews your mind.

> Finally, brethren, whatever things are true, whatever things are noble, whatever things are just, whatever things are pure, whatever things are lovely, whatever things are of good report, if there is any virtue and if there is anything praiseworthy—meditate on these things. The things which you learned and received and heard and saw in me, these do, and the God of peace will be with you.
>
> —PHILIPPIANS 4:8–9

Your attitude is renewed.

> Regarding your former way of life, you were taught to strip off your old nature, which is being ruined by its deceptive desires, to be renewed in your mental attitude.
>
> —EPHESIANS 4:22–23, ISV

You take on Christ's attitude.

> Have this attitude in yourselves which was also in Christ Jesus.
>
> —PHILIPPIANS 2:5, NASB

You put on a new nature.

> Do not lie to one another, since you have put off the old man with his deeds, and have put on the new man who is renewed in knowledge according to the image of Him who created him.
>
> —COLOSSIANS 3:9–10

You're kept in perfect peace.

> You will keep in perfect peace those whose minds are
> steadfast, because they trust in you.
>
> —ISAIAH 26:3, NIV

RENEWING YOUR MIND IS
THE MOST IMPORTANT THING

The most important area to pay attention to and defend is your mind. The habit of renewing your mind will also renew your life! It will help you to continue thinking, speaking, and acting according to the teachings of the Word of God and not according to your emotions and feelings. This will bring you emotional healing, peace, restoration, prosperity, and wisdom to make valuable and life-changing decisions.

The day you believed in Jesus Christ an incredible miracle took place in your heart—you were born again. When that happened, the Spirit of God came into your spirit and restored it to its original design and intention.

The instant you received salvation your spirit was renewed, and you were spiritually awakened to the things of God. But the work of transformation the apostle Paul speaks about is not about your spirit—it refers to your soul and your mind. The mind is the place where the change and transformation must take effect and where you must be conformed to the image of Jesus Christ.

Your soul is where your personality, ego, thoughts, memories, will, emotions, and mind are located. *The entrance to the life of the soul is not the will or the emotions—it is the mind. Every thought passes through the mind.*

If your spirit has been regenerated, but your mind is not renewed, the new life that is in your spirit cannot reach your soul effectively. This is an absolute truth in Scripture. That is why it is emphasized—the mind must be renewed.

Think of it this way: when a person is dominated by a sinful and compulsive desire that he or she cannot overcome, the problem is not in the desire itself—it is in his or her mind.

Your mind must be renewed to be set free from wrong thinking. The Scriptures clearly say that lust is a deceitful and compulsive desire you can't rule and over which you have no control. It is the condition of a darkened and empty mind. If the mind is in darkness, the will is also in darkness, and its desires will overpower it.

> …that you put off, concerning your former conduct, the old man which grows corrupt according to the deceitful lusts, and be renewed in the spirit of your mind, and that you put on the new man which was created according to God, in true righteousness and holiness.
>
> —EPHESIANS 4:22–24

You might be thinking, "Iris, this is great, but how do I know if I am renewing my mind? Is there something I need to do?" The answer is yes, and it is very simple. There are three things you need to do on a daily basis. You should also use these prayers as examples to form your own prayers and allow the Holy Spirit to help you.

1. **Be willing to put off your "old man."** This refers to the "old man" in your mind—all negative and false thoughts, concepts, and beliefs associated with your past and your upbringing.

Dear God, I surrender my life, my past, and my desires to You. I am no longer a slave to sin (Rom. 6:6). Holy Spirit, I am willing to put off all the things in my mind that are hindrances to my spiritual growth and peace of mind. Thank You for Your help. In Jesus' name, amen.

2. **Ask the Holy Spirit for help.** Have intimate fellowship and prayer with Him every day. Don't be afraid to ask for His help and counsel in every area of your life. The Holy Spirit works in us and with us, but never without us. Transformation requires that we allow the Holy Spirit to work in us to teach us an entirely new plan and purpose of spiritual habits.

Holy Spirit, I accept and acknowledge You as my helper. Thank You for teaching me all the things in the Word of God that will transform my life and renew my mind (John 14:26). Help me to pay attention and to desire to spend time with You. God, I thank You for Your Spirit that dwells in me and helps me become stronger each day (1 Cor. 3:16). I am willing to learn from You. Please open my eyes and show me great and wonderful things from Your Word (Ps. 119:18).

3. **Meditate on the Word of God.** God has given us all the spiritual resources necessary to be conformed to the image of His Son. We must cooperate with the Holy Spirit for this change to happen, and we need to meditate on the Word of God habitually. Only the Word of God has the power to reveal and remove from our minds the habits and the thoughts of the old man.

Dear Father God, help me to learn and to meditate upon Your Word day and night and to obey Your counsel (Josh. 1:8). Help me to be still and to trust You with my life and my family (Ps. 4:4).

WHY IS IT IMPORTANT TO
KNOW THE ROLE OF THE MIND?

The mind is the battleground where Satan and his evil spirits fight against the truth.

> For though we walk in the flesh, we do not war according to the flesh. For the weapons of our warfare are not carnal but mighty in God for pulling down strongholds, casting down arguments and every high thing that exalts itself against the knowledge of God, bringing every thought into captivity to the obedience of Christ.
>
> —2 CORINTHIANS 10:3–5

The apostle Paul understood that the battle of the believer takes place in the mind. The mind is the place where Satan lines up all his forces to destroy the children of God. It is the battleground. As we read this passage, we can see the language of spiritual warfare:

- "Weapons of our warfare" (We are in a battle, and we have weapons.)

- "Bringing every thought into captivity to the obedience of Christ" (specific instruction on how to wage spiritual warfare)

- "Pulling down strongholds, casting down arguments" (specific instruction on what things to destroy with prayer and declarations from the Word of God)

It is essential to understand that God wants us to occupy our minds. Many expect God to cleanse their minds of all the bad stuff. But we must do our part in this warfare. Jesus Christ already paid the price for our freedom. God does not erase our minds; He renews them so we can know Him and obey Him. If I do not use my mind, there are occult and demonic beings that are waiting to occupy it.

> *Dear Abba Father, Your Word is powerful and able to cleanse me and renew my mind as I obey it, declare it, and put it into action. I believe that as I obey and pay attention to Your Word, I can say with confidence, "I have the mind of Christ" (1 Cor. 2:16). Help me to study and meditate on the Word so that I will have a Spirit-ruled mind and not a sense-ruled mind. Thank You for this revelation.*

HOW TO WIN THE BATTLE OF THE MIND

The first thing we must understand is the importance of having freedom in our minds to exercise our faith. It is a vital need and necessary to live in freedom and wholeness.

We learn in Proverbs 23:7 that "as [a person] thinks in his heart, so is he." What we think transforms into who we are and how we act and believe. This is a great truth. We must think seriously about this.

We all experience the battle in our minds. We need to understand that this battle is not won in one day; it depends on our commitment to stay connected to the Holy Spirit so that He will be the One guiding us and fighting for us.

You must keep moving forward and continue in the battle without stopping. The renewal of the mind is a process. God fights our battles. We must do the believing and trusting. Every day we have to sow a seed of faith and hurl a declaration of victory at the enemy. Meditating on specific scriptures and making declarations every day are very effective in renewing the mind.

Many times it is possible that thoughts of disbelief will come to our mind. But to renew our minds, we must decide to believe and act on what the living and active Word of God says. Often the

Holy Spirit gives us faith for things that our minds do not always seem able to assimilate. The mind wants to understand everything, but many times the mind refuses to believe what it cannot understand. We must raise the shield of faith and ask God for wisdom in the trials so that He will show us what we need to tear down in prayer.

> *My Lord, I realize the battle for my mind is very serious (1 Pet. 1:13). In Jesus' name I put on the helmet of salvation to cover and protect my mind from all the fiery darts of the enemy, and I put on the shield of faith, making daily confessions of faith (Eph. 6:16–17). Thank You, Father God, for this great privilege.*

Conclusion

Ask God for understanding so that His light will penetrate your mind to help you discover what strongholds the enemy has raised in your mind. Once you take every thought captive, it is easier to filter out every thought according to the Word of God.

You must master your flesh and your attitudes. If you genuinely want to experience the peace of God in your home, renew your understanding with the knowledge of the Word of God and live as God created you to live. Do not walk defeated and unhappy, but walk with the help and the power of the Holy Spirit. You will always have tribulations, but you are not beaten.

God requires a transformation of your life, beginning with your heart by the renewing and teaching of the mind. The Bible does not speak of seeking remedies to improve life but to renew it through knowledge from the Word of God and the teachings of pastors and mentors.

If you commit yourself to renewing your mind through the knowledge of the Word of God, allowing the Holy Spirit to reveal all the things you need to remove from your life, you are going to experience the fullness and victory of new life in Christ Jesus, as well as answered prayers. You must believe this.

> *I faithfully commit to the process of renewing my mind by studying God's Word and putting it into action. Thank You, Holy Spirit, for helping me to be diligent and determined to never give up. In Jesus' name, amen.*

GET TO THE HEART

Use this space to write down insights this chapter has given you on renewing your mind and any prayers or Scripture verses that the Lord has brought to light.

_____

_____

_____

_____

_____

_____

_____

_____

_____

_____

PART II

PROTECT YOUR CHILD

Guard your heart *above all else, for it determines the course of your life.*
—Proverbs 4:23, NLT, emphasis added

Chapter 4

PRAY FOR YOUR CHILD
AT ANY AGE

And in Your book they all were written, the days
fashioned for me, when as yet there were none of them.
—Psalm 139:16

G OD HAS AMAZING plans for our lives and our children's
lives. He wants us to raise up a generation that will
do great things for Him, and it all begins with prayer.
Remember, the prayers throughout this book have been written
to teach you how to pray. Please do not think of them as a script
you have to follow religiously. Like the prayer Jesus prayed during
His Sermon on the Mount, they are a template, or pattern, you
can follow as you develop your own prayer life. Personalize them
by inserting the name of your son, daughter, or loved one in each
prayer. As your child grows, your prayer life will grow too, and you
can use whatever words come from your heart.

**When your child has been conceived (when you become
pregnant)**

> *Dear Father, I thank You for this great promise, that even*
> *before a child is born Your omnipresence and omniscience*
> *are with that baby. Thank You for covering the life of my*

child. Your Word declares, "For You formed my inward parts; You covered me in my mother's womb...My frame was not hidden from You, when I was made in secret, and skillfully wrought in the lowest parts of the earth. Your eyes saw my substance, being yet unformed. And in Your book they all were written, the days fashioned for me, when as yet there were none of them" (Ps. 139:13, 15–16). Father, from the first day, Your eyes have been looking at this child. Thank You for Your divine favor and wisdom to guide every step of my child toward eternal life. In the name of Jesus, amen.

While you are pregnant, I suggest you pray for the child in your womb every day. Be happy, and sing hymns and psalms. Choose and declare some of the declarations in this book. The Spirit of Christ in the fetus receives the messages. Speak words of healing. If a mother is stressed and emotionally frustrated all the time, it is possible that the fetus can sense the same feelings. Take time to rest and meditate on the effects that the Word of God will have in your life and in the life of your baby.

Following are examples of how to pray incredibly important prayers based on promises in God's Word for your children while they are in your womb and when you give birth. Personalize them by placing the name of your child in the prayer.

Dear God, I believe this child will be taught by the Lord and great shall be his/her peace (Isa. 54:13).

My God, protect and fill the heart of my child with Your Word so that he/she will never sin against You (Ps. 119:11).

Father, fill my child with the knowledge of Your will in all wisdom and spiritual understanding so that his/her life will always please You and bear good fruit (Col. 1:9–10).

Dear Lord, my prayer is that my child's heart and understanding are filled with the spirit of wisdom and revelation in the knowledge of Christ so that he/she will always be conscious of his/her calling and inheritance in Christ Jesus (Eph. 1:17–19).

Jehovah God, help my child to trust in You wholeheartedly and never to depend on human understanding (Prov. 3:5–6).

Thank You, Abba Father, for surrounding my child with Your shield of protection and great favor wherever he/she may go. Thank You for Your blessing upon his/her life (Ps. 5:12).

Help my child, dear God, not to worry or fear different circumstances but to remain anchored in Your Word, knowing that Your peace will guard his/her heart and mind in Christ Jesus (Phil. 4:6–9).

When your child is about to be born

Dear Father, You see my condition. Your Word declares, "The LORD will perfect that which concerns me; Your mercy, O LORD, endures forever; do not forsake the works of Your hands" (Ps. 138:8).

I believe this promise for my child who is about to be born and for me. Thank You, Father, for Your peace deep in my heart throughout the birthing process. Cover us with the powerful blood of Jesus. I thank You for Your angels who will be attentive to all the details. Bless the hands of the doctors and nurses who will be assisting. Thank You for a completely healthy child who is full of life. Thank You for guarding my body and mind. I cast out all fear and negative thoughts from my mind and my heart. I place my trust in You. In Jesus' name, amen.

When your pastor presents your child before God and the church

Dear Father, today we give You thanks for Your love and Your blessings in our lives. Thank You for this privilege to dedicate this child in Your presence in the same way that Jesus was presented in the temple eight days after His birth. Help us as parents to commit ourselves to guiding this child in the teaching and admonition of the Word and in the fear of the Lord. Thank You, my God, for imparting Your blessing over our family. In the name of our Lord Jesus Christ, amen.

As you begin parenting

When children are young, they are more willing and susceptible to believe what the Bible says about love, forgiveness, and the presence of God. It is very important to emphasize love as we care for their physical needs, and we must present the plan of salvation to them. Don't be afraid to be specific, and at the same time make it fun by relating Bible stories such as David and Goliath, which teach them very important values that will become part of their character and personality.

Father, Your Word declares, "Train up a child in the way he should go, and when he is old, he will not depart from it" (Prov. 22:6). Help me as a parent never to take this responsibility as a sacrifice, but as an urgent necessity. Fill me with Your wisdom and knowledge to always be alert to the wiles of the enemy against my child. As my family grows, help me to bear in mind the importance of building a solid foundation of Your love and Your Word in the hearts of my children. Although the storms come, the foundation will remain firm, and Your promises will be fulfilled in their lives. Thank You, Lord, for Your wisdom, understanding, and knowledge in my life for this crucial task. In the name of Jesus, amen.

When your child is young

Parents, remember that this is a very impressionable age. It is an age when they learn to repeat, memorize, and keep in their hearts the things they see, hear, and learn. Proverbs 22:6 is a promise from God for every parent. No matter the age of a person, if he or she received Jesus in his or her heart during childhood, we must believe that sooner or later he or she will follow the ways of God.

Lord, I thank You for the life of my children. I am certain that You are forming them according to Your heart, mind, and character. I ask that You cover them with Your precious blood and with Your armor. Please remove from their path every person or situation that might impede their fulfilling their divine purpose. Instill in them a mind capable of learning, understanding, and retaining all academic things and all spiritual things.

Remove from their minds all thoughts of "I can't" or "I don't know how," and place in their minds and hearts the conviction of being brave and courageous, trusting that Your Spirit lives in them and equips them for all they are called to do. I bless the lives of my children in the name that is above all names, Jesus Christ. Amen.

As your child goes to school

Lord, please put in my children minds capable of understanding and retaining academic and spiritual things. Guide them by Your Holy Spirit every moment, and fill them with discernment to make every decision today. Let them be found ten times better because Your Holy Spirit is guiding them. Guard their thoughts against being distracted by the things of the world. I bless my children and declare the peace of God over their lives.

Thank You, Father, for keeping them from every relationship that is evil and designed by the enemy to make them stumble. I thank You for the hedge of protection that is continuously around them. I ask that You give them the wisdom to choose their friends and that they always have the fear of God to choose between good and evil. Holy Spirit, help my children to develop good habits in every area of their lives. I thank You for Your blessing over their lives. In the name of Jesus, amen.

When your child is preadolescent or a young teen

It is important to prepare your children for the changes that will take place during their adolescent years, and please have no anxiety or fear of dealing with the issue of their sexuality. Adolescents rapidly change when they enter puberty. During this stage they tend to argue and discuss issues that affect you directly.

This is the precise time in the life of a teenager to hear the truth of the gospel and the struggle between the kingdom of God and the kingdom of Satan. It should be done in an interesting and easy-to-understand manner. Teach your child to fear and respect God and the benefits and blessings that will be part of his or her life forever. Don't miss this vital opportunity to impress your child positively and leave a legacy of blessing.

Lord my God, help me to be a role model of Your love and compassion, especially during the storms and trials. Let my children see Your peace, love, and self-control in me. Give me wisdom and original ideas to teach the precepts in Your Word and explain the war between light and darkness. Thank You, Father, for filling my heart with Your love and wisdom so that I will never lose the urgency of raising my children to have a deep sense of respect and awe for God.

When your child is a young adult

The age of sixteen and older is a stage where friendships and temptations play a significant and dominant role in their lives. The prayers and spiritual vigilance of parents must be a priority. Do not ignore spending family time and offering to help in their studies and personal matters. At this age you can stop parenting and develop a healthy and loving friendship with your children.

> Lord, I thank You for the lives of my children. I pray that You will fill my children with Your grace, favor, and wisdom. Thank You for indwelling them with Your knowledge and understanding to overcome and excel in their tasks and responsibilities. Thank You because You are causing their lives, hearts, minds, and characters to conform to Your likeness.
>
> I pray that on this day, You protect them from all accidents, mechanical failure, and all theft. Thank You for guarding my children against all disease and pestilence. Thank You for covering them with Your precious blood and Your armor. I ask You, dear Father, to remove from their paths every person and hindrance the enemy might use to distract them and lead them away from Your purpose for their lives, and I thank You for giving Your angels charge over them. In the name of Jesus, amen. (Read and study Psalm 91.)

For your child's career and work ethics

Dear Father, You know the hearts of my children and the obstacles that can arise in life. I put their profession and employment in Your hands. Protect them from errors and any external influence of evil that may try to obstruct Your blessing in their lives. Help them to perform with excellence in their workplace and to earn a fair wage. Help them to be free from the bondage of debt and to be consistent, cheerful givers. Thank You, my God, for imparting upon them Your wisdom and understanding (Dan. 2:21).

For your child's dating years

Dear Father, help my children to be patient while they wait for the spouse that You have predestined for them. Protect their minds from all temptation and persuasion of the enemy. Holy Spirit, help them to remain pure until they marry. Your Word says that no matter how great the temptation may be, You make a way out of the temptation.

Prepare them for the married life, that they may choose with prudence, wisdom, understanding, and discernment the right person according to Your will. Help me to give sound counsel with understanding. I thank You for keeping their souls and protecting their minds. In the name of Jesus, amen.

For your child's marriage

Lord my God, I pray my children will be faithful in their marriage. I pray that their love will be without pretension and they will learn to love each other with genuine affection and will delight in honoring each other

(Rom. 12:9–11). *Teach me never to intervene in their marriage or try to dominate or be a hindrance. I thank You for giving wisdom and love that endures. In the name of Jesus, amen.*

When your child becomes a parent

Abba Father, You know the perverse condition of this world and the millions of broken families with sad and neglected children. I pray for my children when they become parents, that they will never stray from Your ways and their hearts will always turn toward their children with good counsel, full of the wisdom of Your Word. Help me to be an example of Your love so they can also learn to raise their children with discipline and instruction that comes from the Lord. Thank You, Father, for this great blessing. I declare that my children and my (future) grandchildren will never stray from the ways of the Lord (Luke 1:17; Eph. 6:4). In Jesus' name, amen.

No legacy more valuable and lasting can we leave to our children than the person of Jesus Christ and a genuine relationship with the Holy Spirit as they grow and mature through the seasons of life. As you move on to the next chapter and discover prayers that transform your child's heart with godly character and values, continue to pray prayers like these, believing that your children belong to the kingdom of God. Even if you don't see any specific changes, keep praying because your prayers are seeds that, at the appointed time, will blossom and bear fruit because each of these truths is based on Scripture.

GET TO THE HEART

Use this space to write down your child's age, what you are specifically praying for that child, and any Scripture verses the Lord is bringing to your mind as you pray.

_____

_____

_____

_____

_____

_____

_____

_____

_____

_____

_____

_____

Chapter 5

TRANSFORM YOUR
CHILD'S HEART

For the word of God is living and powerful, and sharper
than any two-edged sword, piercing even to the division
of soul and spirit, and of joints and marrow, and is a
discerner of the thoughts and intents of the heart.
—HEBREWS 4:12

I BELIEVE THAT PRAYERS like the ones I've modeled for you
throughout this book are the most important and effective
prayers you can pray because they are rooted in the Word
of God. John 1:1 says, "In the beginning was the Word, and the
Word was with God, and the Word was God." Second Timothy
3:16–17 says, "All Scripture is given by inspiration of God, and
is profitable for doctrine, for reproof, for correction, for instruction in righteousness, that the man of God may be complete, thor-
oughly equipped for every good work."

As you can see, our prayers and godly instruction, based on the
Word of God, can make our children capable of every good work.
The following examples of how to pray the Scriptures are powerful.
Whether you pray these exact scriptures or similar ones, pray them
powerfully, believing in faith as the Holy Spirit strengthens and
supports you in the inner man with supernatural power (Eph. 3:16).

PRAYERS TO FORM CHARACTER AND PURPOSE IN YOUR CHILD

To have salvation

Father, draw my children to Jesus Christ from an early age, and cause them to seek You always (2 Chron. 34:1–3; Acts 2:21).

To grow in wisdom

Lord, cause them to grow in wisdom and favor with You and others, just as Jesus "grew in wisdom and stature, and in favor with God and man" (Luke 2:52, NIV).

To have honor and integrity

Father, I pray that my children will honor You with all their substance and walk securely with integrity (Prov. 3:9; 10:9).

To walk in humility and the fear of the Lord

Thank You, Father, for helping my children to walk in humility and the fear of the Lord. Your Word declares in Proverbs 22:4 that in doing so, they will enjoy riches and honor and life.

To have discipline and self-control

Lord, I pray that my children will always demonstrate discipline and self-control in all they do. May they always love to do what is good and pleasing to You and to others (Titus 1:8).

To be peacemakers

Lord, instill in my children the desire to be peacemakers, especially in difficult situations. Help me to be an example of Your peace and dependence upon Your Word so that we might "reap a harvest of righteousness" (Jas. 3:18, NIV).

To have sexual purity

Father, help my children as well as their future spouses to stay pure until marriage. Help them to understand that their bodies are the temple of the Holy Spirit and that their willingness to abstain from immorality will bring honor to God (1 Cor. 6:18–20).

To develop a desire to pray

Thank You, Holy Spirit, for helping my children develop a desire to be faithful in prayer and to learn to seek You first whenever they face anxiety or a special need (Rom. 12:12; Phil. 4:6).

To submit to God

Lord, help my children to completely submit themselves to You and to resist Satan (Jas. 4:7).

To depend on the Holy Spirit for help and guidance

Holy Spirit, I pray that my children will always call upon You for help and divine guidance. May they develop a close and intimate relationship with You (John 14:16–17).

To develop a thankful and grateful spirit

Lord, help my children choose to always be thankful and grateful to You and to others. May they focus on all Your blessings with a thankful heart and be ready to also bless those in need. May Your peace always rule in their hearts with a thankful attitude (Col. 3:15; Eph. 5:20; 1 Thess. 5:18).

To love with a pure heart

Lord, help my children to love with a pure heart from a good conscience and sincere faith. Help me to always be an example of Your love and peace (1 Tim. 1:5).

To resist temptation

Dear Father, help my children to resist temptation and always remember that when they are tempted, You will always provide a way out so they can endure it (1 Cor. 10:13). Thank You for this promise.

To be teachable and truthful

Lord, help my children to be willing to obey Your commandments and to develop a truthful understanding of Christ Jesus. Help them to align themselves with the truth and to forsake all falsehood, insincerity, and lies of the enemy (Prov. 12:1; John 14:6; Heb. 13:15).

To trust God always

Father, I pray that my children will develop a deep intimacy with You and trust Your Word. I pray they will have confidence in knowing that the Lord is their Shepherd, leading them in paths of righteousness (Ps. 23).

To be content and joyful

My Lord, help my children understand and know that they can be content in every situation, no matter what it may be. Help them to develop confidence and satisfaction, not from what they can see, but from a deep knowing of Your love and Your faithful promises to them (Heb. 12:1–2; 13:5).

To do all things without complaining

Lord, place in my children the desire to do all things without complaining and disputing, that they may be found blameless and harmless in the midst of a perverse generation (Phil. 2:14–15).

To be willing to work and be fruitful

Thank You, Father, for helping my children walk worthy of their salvation, bearing fruit in every good work and growing in Your knowledge (Col. 1:10).

To avoid envy

Lord, help my children to avoid being envious of evil people or of their friends. Help them to walk in peace and love, never conceited or provoked by envy (Prov. 24:1; Gal. 5:26).

To never hold a grudge

Father God, please help my children to never seek revenge or bear a grudge against anyone, but I pray they will always be willing to love their neighbor as themselves (Lev. 19:18).

To be forgiving and compassionate

Thank You, my Lord, for helping my children to be kind and compassionate to others, always willing to forgive, just as Christ forgave us (Eph. 4:32).

To desire to know the Word of God

My Lord, help me to be a consistent example of studying and acting upon Your Word so that my children also will develop a desire to study, read, and obey Your Word (Heb. 4:12).

To have perseverance and self-control

Holy Spirit, teach my children to persevere in their Christian walk, always bringing honor to God and exercising self-control in every area of their personal and social lives (2 Pet. 1:6).

To be faithful servants

Dear God, I pray my children will develop the heart of a faithful servant, willing to be truthful in all things and pleasing You in all their ways (Matt. 25:23).

To show gentleness and respect

My Lord, I pray that my children will always desire to be gentle and respectful when asked about their faith in Christ. May they never be ashamed of the gospel, but may they remain secure in their salvation and happy to defend it (Rom. 1:16).

To have a courageous spirit

> *Father, cause the lives of my children to be marked by a courageous spirit, ready to obey Your Word and never turn from it. Do not allow any person or friend to steer them away from the truth* (Josh. 1:7).

To resist the devil

> *Lord, thank You for helping my children become fearless and able to resist the devil. May they never be afraid to call upon You for help. May they always remember that greater is Christ in us than the enemy in the world* (Jas. 4:7; 1 John 4:4).

TWO POWERFUL SCRIPTURES TO PRAY FOR YOUR CHILD EVERY DAY

Place the name of your son or daughter in these two Scripture-based prayers, and try to pray them every day, no matter what you see, know, or hear in their lives. Do it, believing in faith! As you can see reading the scriptures I've placed directly after each prayer, these are not my words; they are powerful prayers directly from the Word of God.

> *Dear God, help me to never cease praying for my children. My prayer is that You will fill them with the knowledge of Your will in all wisdom and spiritual intelligence so they may walk in a manner worthy of You, pleasing You in everything, bearing fruit in every good work, and growing in the knowledge of You. I pray that they will be strengthened according to Your glorious power so that they may obtain strength and perseverance and with joy give thanks to You, the Father, who enables us to participate in Your inheritance.*

For this reason we also, since the day we heard it, do not cease to pray for you, and to ask that you may be filled with the knowledge of His will in all wisdom and spiritual understanding; that you may walk worthy of the Lord, fully pleasing Him, being fruitful in every good work and increasing in the knowledge of God; strengthened with all might, according to His glorious power, for all patience and longsuffering with joy; giving thanks to the Father who has qualified us to be partakers of the inheritance of the saints in the light.

—COLOSSIANS 1:9–12

Dear God, I will never cease to thank You for the lives of my children. Help me to raise them to Your presence constantly in my prayers so that You, the God of our Lord Jesus Christ, the Father of glory, will give them the spirit of wisdom and revelation in the knowledge of You, and that You will open the eyes of their understanding so they may know the hope of Your calling and the riches of the glory of Your inheritance.

[I] do not cease to give thanks for you, making mention of you in my prayers: that the God of our Lord Jesus Christ, the Father of glory, may give to you the spirit of wisdom and revelation in the knowledge of Him, the eyes of your understanding being enlightened; that you may know what is the hope of His calling, what are the riches of the glory of His inheritance in the saints.

—EPHESIANS 1:16–18

Prayers to Transform the Heart of Your Child

To produce the fruit of the Holy Spirit

Thank You, heavenly Father, for manifesting the fruit of the Holy Spirit in the lives of my children. I declare by faith that my children daily demonstrate this fruit, according to Galatians 5:22–23: love, joy, peace, patience, kindness, mercy, good character, obedience, and discretion. Help me, Father, to be a living example of each of these attributes so they form my character and that of my children. In the name of Jesus, amen.

To be guided by the Holy Spirit

I ask You, dear Father, to protect my children from any relationship that is not Your will for them. Holy Spirit, please direct their steps and reveal Yourself to them, impacting their minds and hearts during their sleep. Arouse in them the desire to serve You with all their heart and seek Your help every day (Ps. 119:63; John 15:13–14).

Thank You, Holy Spirit, for guiding my children toward good friendships and keeping their hearts from all corruption, temptation, and lies of the enemy. Teach me, Holy Spirit, to pray specifically for them. Help me to remain vigilant and full of Your Word and powerful prayers. In the name of Jesus Christ, amen (1 Pet. 5:8).

To be obedient to authority

Dear Father, I ask You to help my children to respect and obey any legitimate authority over their lives, observing established laws and showing respect to those who enforce them. Help them never to bend their knee to other gods or agree with anything that is against Your will and Your Word. Fill them with knowledge to understand when they are being directed toward the things of the world and evil. Thank You, Father, because Your promises never change. In the name of Jesus, amen (Rom. 13:1–7; Deut. 7:4; 11:16; Ps. 16:4).

To be obedient and respectful to their parents

Dear Father, guard the hearts of my children and help them to be obedient and respectful toward their parents. Put in them the spirit of discernment to be aware of the enemy's evil tactics against them. Help me to be a living example of Your love and patience toward us. Thank You for saving my children from every attack of the enemy and from all confusion. In the name of Jesus, amen (Col. 3:20; Ps. 119:125; 1 Cor. 14:33).

To be generous and giving

Thank You, my God, for helping us to be faithful in our offerings and tithes and generous with our money and all Your blessings toward us. Help me to be a faithful example so that my children can also follow the example of always being generous with their money and all Your blessings. In the name of Jesus, amen (Prov. 11:25; 22:9).

To be compassionate and merciful

My Lord, touch the hearts of my children so they may always be compassionate toward the poor and destitute. May they never go by the side of a poor person without paying attention and having the compassion to extend their helping hands. May they always sow offerings for the poor with wisdom and understanding. Thank You, Father, for blessing our lives so we can also be blessings to others (Col. 3:12).

To be protected by warrior angels

My Father, thank You for Your warrior angels who are always available to help us and protect us from all evil and all danger. I ask You to cover my children with the protection of the blood of Jesus, and I thank You for sending Your angels to accompany them and defend them in all their ways (Ps. 91:11–12).

To have visions and dreams

Holy Spirit, I ask You to touch my children while they sleep and reveal Yourself to them in powerful visions that transform their lives forever. I declare that my children belong to the kingdom of God and no weapon formed against them will prosper. In the name of Jesus, amen (Dan. 1:17; Acts 2:17; Isa. 54:17).

To be protected from perversion

Father, I thank You for protecting my children's hearts from temptation and perversion. Help them, Holy Spirit, to discern between good and evil. I cover them with the blood of Jesus Christ and bind every spirit of rebellion from attacking their minds. Thank You, Father God, for saving my children from all perversion and every strategy of the enemy. I declare that my children are heirs of the kingdom of God (1 Cor. 10:13; Amos 5:14; Rom. 8:17).

To be protected from sexual harassment

Lord, thank You for protecting my children from every diabolical plan of the enemy to seduce or force them to do immoral acts against their will. Thank You for stopping the enemy's hand against them in every adverse situation. Protect them from all acts of sexual perversion from friends, family, and strangers. I am confident that no weapon formed against them will prevail. In the name of Jesus, amen (John 17:15; 1 Cor. 6:18–20; Isa. 54:17).

To be protected while they sleep

Thank You, Father, for Your divine protection over my children while they sleep. I ask You, Holy Spirit, to invade their minds with life-transforming understanding and insight that will affect their thoughts and actions. Fill them with wisdom to make right decisions when they are awake. In the name of Jesus, amen (Prov. 3:24; 16:3; Heb. 4:12).

Nothing is impossible for God Almighty. King David knew that his prayers were meaningful and powerful. He prayed specifically for his son Solomon, believing that God Almighty was very attentive to his prayers and ready to act upon his faith. His son Solomon ended up becoming king and the richest man on earth during his time. He was also known for his wisdom and prolific writings in the Book of Proverbs. I highly recommend that you also pray this prayer with boldness and genuine faith, no matter what age your son or daughter may be, and that you encourage him or her to read one chapter of Proverbs every day to build up faith and gain wisdom to make brilliant decisions:

My dear God, give my son/daughter an uncluttered and focused heart so that he/she can obey what You command, live by Your directions and counsel, and carry through with the plan You have already predestined for his/her life (1 Chron. 29:19, MSG).

You will be surprised at all the divine intervention available for you and your children when you seek it and pray for help.

GET TO THE HEART

Use this space to write down the specific godly traits you are praying to see in your child and any prayers or Scripture verses the Lord is bringing to your mind as you pray.

_____

_____

_____

_____

_____

_____

_____

_____

_____

_____

Chapter 6

PROTECT YOUR CHILD'S BODY, MIND, SOUL, AND SPIRIT

He sent out his word and healed them, snatching them from the door of death. Let them praise the LORD for his great love and for the wonderful things he has done for them.
—PSALM 107:20–21, NLT

IN THIS CHAPTER I will provide you with prayers for children in need of healing. These prayers will target children experiencing attention and learning difficulties, challenging behavior, autism, confusion in their identity, anxiety, depression, suicidal thoughts, and mental disorders. If your child has been diagnosed with some type of mental illness, or you notice some of these traits and unusual behaviors, I want you to understand that my purpose is not to deny the diagnosis. I want to open your understanding so you receive faith and encouragement to make powerful and specific prayers that can destroy the roots of all diseases, disorders, disobedience, confusion, and mental attacks of the enemy and reverse a diagnosis made by doctors and specialists.

The following statistics will give you an idea of the high prevalence of fatherlessness in many homes across our nation and the dangerous trends now taking place in our society. If there's any doubt that divorce leaves deep, lasting scars, consider these alarming numbers from Fatherhood.org: one in four children in the United States now lives without a father in the home. That's more than nineteen million US children living without a biological, step, or adoptive father. Kids in fatherless homes are

+ seven times more likely to become pregnant as a teen;

+ four times more likely to face poverty;

+ twice as likely to drop out of high school;

+ twice as likely to suffer obesity.[1]

In addition, Fatherhood.org says that children in fatherless homes are more likely to face abuse and neglect, experience behavioral problems, abuse drugs and alcohol, commit crime, and go to prison.

Next to depression, anxiety disorders are among the most common mental health illnesses in young people. Anxiety disorders can include phobias, obsessive-compulsive disorder, panic attacks, social anxiety, and post-traumatic stress. It's estimated that 10 percent of teens may be suffering from one or more of these conditions.[2]

Depression might be diagnosed if someone has at least five of the following symptoms:

+ Mood disorder, hopelessness, and distrust

+ Loss of appetite or overindulging

+ Eating disorders that become untreatable

+ Impatience, restlessness

+ Exhaustion, tiredness

+ Suicidal feelings and attempts

+ Inability to think clearly, focus, or remember details

+ Constant headaches, aches, or contractions

+ Sleeplessness or too much sleep

+ Constant feelings of sadness and apprehension

+ Feelings of wrongdoing, insignificance, and powerlessness

+ Anxiety disorder, panic disorder, and phobias

According to many research statistics, there are millions of US children with some type of serious mental illness that may significantly hinder their daily lives.[3]

WHAT ARE THE SYMPTOMS OF MENTAL ILLNESS IN CHILDREN?

Symptoms in children vary, depending on the type of mental illness, but some of the general symptoms include:

+ Constant fear and dismay

+ Withdrawal from family and friends

+ Strange, erratic behavior

+ A decline in self-care and personal hygiene and appearance

+ Spending of an excessive, unusual amount of time alone

+ A significant drop in grades or job performance

+ Strong inappropriate emotions or a loss of feelings

+ Constant outbursts of anger

+ A suspiciousness of others

+ Nightmares and sleeplessness

+ A lack of motivation

+ Constant irritability and aggression

+ Substance abuse

+ Hyperactive behavior, hallucinations[4]

BEWARE OF THE IDENTITY CRISIS AFFECTING THIS GENERATION

You may not have had to confront the serious problem of identity crisis or gender confusion among your family members yet, but let me warn you that it has become an enormous problem among many families, including Christian families. Your children might not talk about this subject, but they are very aware that it is going on all around them. Our teenagers are being greatly deceived by the enemy, who is doing everything he can to distract our children from achieving their destiny in Christ Jesus.

Identity crisis will take the form of insecurity, fear, rejection, doubt, and unhappiness. The enemy will use all these emotions to bring confusion to their very identity as a male or female. The Word of God is very clear: "So God created man in His own image; in the image of God He created him; male and female He created them" (Gen. 1:27); "But from the beginning of the creation, God 'made them male and female'" (Mark 10:6).

Parents, be aware that you are in a constant spiritual war for the souls of your loved ones. Learn to pray powerfully and with a set target. Ask the Holy Spirit to give you discernment to understand right from wrong and to discern demonic intrusion when it tries to attack your children. Yes, they will face many trials and challenges from their peers and friends, and you must be prepared to confront and challenge every lie of hell. Always remember, "God is not the author of confusion but of peace" (1 Cor. 14:33).

It is imperative to reassure your children that they are loved and they belong to God. You must also teach them from an early age about good and evil and about their identity in Christ Jesus. Make sure you teach your young children the basics about God's Word. Remember, Proverbs 22:6 tells you to train your child in the way he or she should go so when your child is old, he or she won't depart from it. This verse contains a promise that no matter which path your child is following right now, as long as you trained your child in the way of the Lord, he or she will not depart from that training. Praise God!

You must also learn to depend on the Holy Spirit for daily guidance so that you will learn how to answer difficult questions when they arise and discern the intrusion of the enemy at all times.

The most important thing you can do is teach your children the Word of God at an early age. Get them into a church that values children and always has the Word of God in front of them in all forms (Sunday school lessons, skits, programs, entertaining formats, etc.), and make sure they memorize and remember scriptures. God's Word is alive and active!

If you're saying, "I've done all these things, Mrs. Delgado, but my child still has a huge problem. They're telling me they are depressed, being harassed by their friends, rejected, angry, and confused about their identity. What can I do?" Get help! Find a good counselor. Talk frankly to your pastor. Don't hide it! Ask God to direct your path. Be deliberate and truthful. If your child is struggling with gender identity or homosexuality, open your Bible and show your child the verses about sexuality. Don't avoid a discussion.

Your Child's Identity in Christ Jesus

Memorize and meditate on each of the following truths until it becomes part of your personality and that of your children. It is also very effective to place the name of your child or grandchild in front of each declaration. Make a habit of saying faith declarations such as these every day. For example: "My daughter Kathy is a child of the living God, and she's an heir of God and a joint heir with Christ Jesus!" This practice will become a very dynamic and effective exercise. Here are more examples of declarations you can make about your child's identity in Christ:

- My child is a child of God (Rom. 8:14–15).

- My child is an heir of God and a joint heir with Christ Jesus (Rom. 8:17).

- My child is holy and sanctified in Christ (1 Cor. 1:2).

- My child has been justified and redeemed (Rom. 3:24).

- My child has the mind of Christ (1 Cor. 2:16).

- The Holy Spirit dwells in my child (1 Cor. 3:16; 6:19).

- My child is established and anointed and sealed in Christ (2 Cor. 1:21–22).

- My child is a new creation (2 Cor. 5:17).

- My child has been redeemed and forgiven and has God's wisdom and understanding (Eph. 1:7–8).

- My child has been released from the domain of darkness into the kingdom of Christ (Col. 1:13).

- My child is a child of light and not of darkness (1 Thess. 5:5).

- My child is an enemy of the devil (1 Pet. 5:8).

- My child is loved by the Father (1 John 3:1).

CHILDREN WHO NEED MENTAL AND EMOTIONAL HEALING

Many events and situations can cause a broken heart in a human being. Divorce can be a devastating tragedy for children. Other situations can cause a broken heart in a child, such as physical and mental abuse, rejection, abandonment, attempted abortion before birth, hatred, or the death of a loved one, among other things. Some children never overcome the heartbreak and pain caused by these experiences. They remain broken and unhappy adults until they receive healing and divine intervention.

We cannot diminish the important role that forgiveness plays in the healing of a wounded heart, especially of a child or youngster. Love and powerful, targeted prayers are the most effective medicine to heal a wounded and broken heart. Make a habit of covering your family, your mind, your home, and your property with prayers and declarations of faith every day, and apply the powerful blood of Jesus Christ over them.

This is very important advice that I practice every day, in the morning and in the evening. It is a necessary habit, equal to feeding your body and going to work. The enemy is always looking for passive Christians who do not pray so he might steal their blessings. Besides praying, also manifest your love with hugs, kisses, smiles, and words of encouragement.

I realize I have included quite a bit of information in this chapter. I believe protecting children's mental and emotional health is becoming a tremendous challenge for many parents. I receive prayer requests all the time for children going through depression and experiencing suicidal thoughts.

I also believe that the Word of God is alive and active and powerful to tear down strongholds and set your children free. Go through this chapter and highlight the prayers that minister to you and that you believe will help your children come out of depression and every attack of the enemy against them. Declare the following prayers every day without doubting. You must be bold and determined to stand firm upon God's Word. You will have the victory if you remain steadfast and positive.

Physical, emotional, and mental well-being

Father, I ask You to please touch my children's bodies, minds, and hearts. I declare in faith that my children belong to the kingdom of God and Satan cannot overcome in their lives. Thank You, Father, for saving them from destruction and a life without direction. No weapon formed against them will prosper, in Jesus' name!

My Lord God, Your Word gives us counsel not to be anxious but to present our requests before You in prayer with thanksgiving (Phil. 4:6–7). I thank You for Your peace and for keeping my heart and my thoughts during this time of great trials with my children. I surrender them to Your presence, and I believe in my heart that You hear my prayers and You are aware of their coming in and going out. I have faith that soon You will open a door for their healing and complete restoration of all sickness and attacks of the enemy against their lives. My Lord, Your Word says that all who had ailments—those afflicted by various diseases and torments, the demon-possessed, epileptics, and paralytics—were brought to You, and You healed them (Matt. 4:24).

I believe in my heart that You still listen to the requests and prayers of Your children and that You hear us and are ready to heal us. I thank You for the healing of my children. I lift them up before Your presence, and I pray, believing that You will bring them out of the enemy's land completely restored.

Teach me, Holy Spirit, to keep myself anchored in the Word and not allow my faith to become weak. In the name of Jesus I bind every spirit of rebellion and confusion in my children, and I command the blinders on their eyes to come off. In Jesus' name, amen!

Brokenheartedness

Dear Father, Your Word declares that when the righteous cry out, the Lord hears and delivers them out of all their troubles and that Jehovah is close to the brokenhearted and saves them and protects all their bones so that none of them are broken (Ps. 34:17–20).

Mental illness

Beloved Father, Your Word declares that Jesus healed those who were tormented by demons, and they left with a healthy mind (Luke 8:35). I stand in the gap for my child, and I thank You for touching and healing his/her mind and freeing it from all false teaching and all diabolical influence. Father, Your Son Jesus shed His blood on the cross of Calvary to set us free from all sin, sickness, and attacks of the enemy. Father, thank You for the authority and promise You have given us to trample and defeat evil spirits, and over all the power of the enemy. Nothing shall by any means hurt us (Luke 10:19). In Jesus' name I command every evil spirit to come out and release my loved one. Thank You, Father, for this miracle.

Nightmares

Lord Jesus, You are the Prince of Peace. I pray that You would cover my children with Your protection and send Your angels to encamp around them and keep them from all harm and from the harassment of evil spirits. I release them from all tormenting bad dreams and nightmares, and I declare Your Word in Psalm 4:8: "In peace I will lie down and sleep, for you alone, LORD, make me dwell in safety" (NIV). I command all evil spirits to leave my child and my home in the name of Jesus. I claim victory and stand in faith, believing God's Word in Proverbs 3:24: "When you lie down, you will not be afraid; when you lie down, your sleep will be sweet" (NIV). Thank You, Father God, for this great promise.

Fear

Father, I thank You because I know that Your angels defend and accompany my children in all their ways. I will fear no evil, and in the name of Jesus I stand in the gap, trusting that the peace of God guards their hearts and protects their bodies and minds. As Your Word declares, "The angel of the LORD encamps all around those who fear Him, and delivers them" (Ps. 34:7).

Worry and anxiety

Father, I believe that Your promises are true and are for all Your children. Your Word declares that You will keep in perfect peace the person whose mind is stayed on You because he/she trusts You (Isa. 26:3). I ask that You fill my child's heart with Your peace and that You help him/ her to rely completely on You. In the name of Jesus I cast out every spirit of worry and anxiety from my child's heart. As Your Word declares, "God has not given us a spirit of fear, but of power and of love and of a sound mind" (2 Tim. 1:7).

Sickness

Lord, Your Word declares that You heal all our sicknesses and You redeem our lives from destruction. Jesus was wounded and afflicted; He took our diseases and suffered our pains, and by His stripes we were healed. I am thankful for such an immense sacrifice, and I believe and confess my healing and my children's healing in the name of Jesus (Ps. 103:1–5; Isa. 53:4–5; Matt. 8:17).

Long-term illness

In the name of Jesus I bind every spirit of infirmity attacking my child's body, and I cast it out. I release the healing power of Jesus Christ to touch my child's body right now. By the shed blood of Jesus Christ, I believe my child is healed (Isa. 53:5). Thank You, Father God, for this precious gift. In the name of Jesus, amen.

When a child is going astray

My Father, I believe Your Word in 2 Timothy 1:7, where it says, "For God has not given us a spirit of fear, but of power and of love and of a sound mind." Guard my heart against negative spirits, dear God, as I stand firm upon Your Word and Your promises. I declare and firmly believe that I will see my children return from the enemy's camp. In the name of Jesus I bind every lying spirit of the enemy operating in their lives, and I release the truth of God and the spirit of understanding to penetrate their minds and transform their hearts.

Thank You, Father God, for raising intercessors on behalf of my children and sending ministering angels to minister to their lives. Thank You for the miracles I will see. In the name of Jesus, amen!

My almighty God, I stand firm upon Your words of encouragement in Isaiah 41:10, where You instruct me not to fear because You are with me, not to be dismayed because You are my God and You strengthen my children and me. You will always help us and sustain us with Your righteous right hand. Thank You for this great promise for my children, even if they are out of Your fold at this time.

I declare in faith that my children belong to the kingdom of God and the enemy cannot enslave them. I apply the blood of Jesus Christ over them, and I thank You, Father, for Your divine protection and guidance in their lives. Thank You for Your mighty warrior angels who are keeping watch over them. I have faith that soon I will see them totally healed and saved. In the name of Jesus, amen!

To protect them from negative words spoken over them

Dear Father, in the name of Jesus I pray that my children awaken to the knowledge and understanding of the liberating power in Jesus Christ. I ask that You save them from every curse and plan of the enemy to destroy their minds and their calling.

Father, Your Word declares in Psalm 107:20 that You have sent Your Word and healed them and delivered them from their destructions. I believe this promise for my children! By faith I declare it done and refuse to doubt or say that they are a lost cause. I believe in the healing power that resides in the blood of Jesus and Your Word. I believe that my children are heirs of the kingdom of God. In the name of Jesus, amen!

Confusion about gender or sexuality

Dear Lord my God, help my children to remain fully conscious and totally convinced of the gender identity God has given them based on their biological gender at birth. Help them to flee from all immorality. I plead the blood of Jesus over them and believe my children belong to God. In Jesus' name, amen!

Dear Father God, please help my children not to be fooled or blinded by the enemy and to understand that those who indulge in immorality and any sex outside of marriage, including fornication and adultery, or who practice homosexuality, will not inherit the kingdom of God (1 Cor. 6:9–10). May they honor You with their bodies because You created them and purchased them at a very high price.

I cover my children with the blood of Jesus Christ and bind the enemy's plans for their destruction. Thank You, Abba Father, for giving me peace and boldness never to doubt Your Word. In the powerful name of Jesus Christ, amen!

Prayer of agreement for your child's healing

Come into agreement with a prayer partner or with the Word of God as you make this prayer for your son or daughter.

Father God, I come with boldness into Your presence. I join in this prayer of agreement with the Word of God [or with your prayer partner], and I bring Isaiah 53:5 to Your memory: "But He was wounded for our transgressions, He was bruised for our iniquities; the chastisement for our peace was upon Him, and by His stripes we are healed."

Father, I believe and enter into agreement because Jesus has paid the price for the healing and restoration of my son/daughter. Father, Your Word says that "the prayer of faith will save the sick, and the Lord will raise him up. And if he has committed sins, he will be forgiven" (Jas. 5:15). You also promise in Exodus 15:26 that You are the Lord who heals us. I come against the afflictions and attacks of the enemy against the body of my son/daughter, and I declare restoration and total healing in his/her body at this moment in the name of Jesus! By faith I claim that he/she is healed! In the name of Jesus I believe that my son/daughter is healed. I believe he/she is healed from [name the specific sickness]. We establish this accord in the name of Jesus. Amen!

Prayer of agreement for your whole family's healing and restoration

Get into agreement, and declare healing for all your family.

Dear Father God, I believe that by the stripes of Jesus we are healed and set free from all demonic oppression. Many of us are standing upon Your Word, believing for miraculous healing and for deliverance and restoration for a family member.

Many of us right now are suffering in pain, some with depression, some with fearful torment of some unfinished business, some with a broken home, some experiencing deep loneliness, some with hurting and abused children, some with sexual addictions, and some have been waiting for specific answers to their prayers.

Lord, I stand in agreement with them, reminding You of Your infallible Word and Your infinite promises. I rebuke sickness and demonic oppression and command the spirits of sickness, disease, fear, torment, and abuse to release the people reading this prayer right now, in the name of Jesus! I speak to their immune systems and command the rebellious cells to die and new, healthy cells to take over.

I speak to their minds and their hearts to receive Your wholeness. Father, I thank You for healing every person who is sincerely standing in agreement with me to receive healing and restoration. In Jesus' name, amen!

GET TO THE HEART

Use this space to write down your child's mental or emotional needs and any prayers or Scripture verses the Lord is bringing to your mind to pray for him or her.

_____

_____

_____

_____

_____

_____

_____

_____

_____

_____

_____

_____

_____

_____

Chapter 7

INVALIDATE THE ATTACKS
OF THE ENEMY

But know this, that in the last days perilous times will come.
—2 Timothy 3:1

THIS GENERATION IS being tossed about like dry leaves in the wind and like uncontrollable waves in the ocean. The minds of our children are being infiltrated by all the latest fads and rebellious lifestyles.

In Judges 2 we see the results of a generation of people who failed to fulfill their responsibility of communicating the Word of God to their children—spiritual, moral, and social decadence. Today we are witnessing the effects of what the Bible calls "the sins of the parents." The Word of God says in Numbers 14:18 that the Lord is merciful and forgives iniquity and sin when there is repentance and forgiveness. But the sin that has not been confessed and forgiven continues from one generation to another. When a Christian parent comes before God and repents and receives God's forgiveness, then the curse is broken and the blessings begin to flow.

Many Christian parents and churches have failed to teach children about the evil dangers bombarding their homes. We are losing many children through social media platforms and television programs that raise an altar of admiration to promiscuity, rebellion, and suicide as a way out of problems, without consequences. Films and video games full of conjuring and demonic invocation that inject our youth with contempt for the holy things and for Jesus Christ are now widely accepted.

The enemy uses social media networks with a very elaborate plan to capture the minds of adolescents and our young people, disrupting communication, unity, and family time. This kind of lifestyle leads only to low self-esteem, anxiety, disillusion, and a lack of ambition to do the things that are really important.

It is time to wake up! There is great urgency to serve God, to teach our children, and to cover them with powerful prayers that will protect their hearts. We need to be vigilant as parents to do whatever it takes to defend our children from the attacks of the enemy. In this chapter I've provided you with powerful examples of how to pray the words of Scripture as protection from the enemy's evil schemes and assignments.

PRAYERS TO INVALIDATE THE ATTACKS OF THE ENEMY

When the enemy creates doubt

The Word says that if I speak to my mountain, and in the name of Jesus I order it to depart, it will move. By faith I believe that nothing is impossible for me. My child will see no doubt or unbelief in my life (Matt. 17:20).

Lord, please forgive my unbelief and help my children never to doubt You. Help them to remain firm, believing in Your Word. Because we walk by faith and not by sight, today I believe my children will make the decision to walk by faith. Thank You, Holy Spirit, for Your help while my children learn to live by faith. In the name of Jesus, amen (Matt. 14:31; 2 Cor. 5:7; Gal. 5:5).

When the enemy causes insomnia

Father, You have promised that if I keep Your Word before my eyes and guard it in my heart, it will be life and health to all my flesh (Prov. 4:20–22). When we lie down to sleep, we will not have fear, and our sleep will be peaceful. I believe this promise for my family and for me, and I order insomnia and restlessness to leave in the name of Jesus (Prov. 3:1–2, 24; Isa. 57:2).

When the enemy creates danger and fear

Father God, I believe that Your angels are positioned all around my entire family to defend us. My children will not fear, because You have given us authority over all the power of the enemy. In the name of Jesus I order fear to depart from my children, and I thank You for Your peace guarding their hearts (Ps. 34:7).

When the enemy causes laziness and distraction in your children

Father, give me the strength to recover my vitality and my energy and to remain focused. I renounce the works of the enemy and declare that my children will not be sluggards or procrastinators. I declare that we are free from curses of idleness (laziness) in the name of Jesus. Amen (Prov. 6:6–11).

When your family's defeat seems imminent

Lord, I stand upon Your Word, convinced that when the enemy plans to defeat my children, You will rush in like a flood, overwhelm the enemy, and convert my children's defeat into a victory. You make them triumph and obtain the victory in Christ Jesus. Thank You for sustaining them during these adverse and difficult circumstances. In the name of Jesus, amen (Isa. 59:19).

When the enemy causes scarcity and lack in your home

Father, I repent from anything I have done or failed to do that has caused insufficiency and lack in my children's lives. Teach me, Holy Spirit, how to put the principle of sowing and reaping into action. In the name of almighty Jesus, I release this curse of shortage and poverty so it will not repeat in my children's lives, and I ask You for wisdom and understanding to be a good steward, obedient to the Word of God. My God shall supply all my needs—and my children's needs—according to His riches in glory by Christ Jesus (Phil. 4:19).

When the enemy causes your child to worry and be anxious

Father, guard my children's hearts, and protect them in Your perfect peace. In the name of Jesus I cast out all worry and anxiousness from their minds and hearts. My children will trust You, Lord. You have not given them a spirit of fear. You have given them power, love, and a sound mind. Thank You for this promise, in the name of Jesus (Isa. 26:3; Phil. 4:6–7; 2 Tim. 1:7).

When the enemy brings opposition in your child's life

Father, Your Word declares that no weapon formed against me shall prosper and that You will condemn every tongue that rises up against me. I declare this promise over my children and my entire family. Thank You for this promise (Isa. 54:17).

When the enemy causes your child to doubt God's love

Father God, thank You for Your gift of love. While my children were still sinners, Christ shed His blood for them. Thank You for this wonderful love that has been poured into their hearts and that continues to sustain them (Rom. 5:8–9).

When the enemy plants seeds of hatred and resentment

Lord, forgive me for harboring feelings of hate and resentment when someone offends my child or me. I repent, and I ask You to have mercy on my enemies. Your Word declares that hatred stirs up strife but love covers all sins. Teach me to cover people—both inside and outside of my home—with love. Thank You for opening my spiritual understanding so I show my child an example of loving forgiveness and not hatred. I declare that this spirit does not have the authority to rule my life or my home (Prov. 10:12).

When the enemy causes weariness and discouragement

Father, thank You because Your Word declares that You give power to the weak and increase strength in those who have no strength. When my children are tired, You make them soar with wings like eagles. I declare that discouragement will not have control over our household (Isa. 40:29–31; Heb. 12:3).

When your family is plagued by lack of self-control

Father, I repent from excessiveness and lack of restraint in my life. Your Word says that a person without self-control is like a broken-down city without walls. Thank You for helping me to exemplify healthy habits for my children that glorify and honor Your name while helping me and my children to feel better and live longer, healthier lives (Prov. 23:2; 25:28; Rom. 14:17).

When someone in your home has suicidal tendencies

Father, You formed my child in the womb with a purpose and a defined destiny. Satan comes to steal, kill, and destroy, but You come to give life in abundance. I declare that my children belong to You and that no weapon formed against them shall prosper. In the name of Jesus I bind the spirit of suicide and cast it out of my life and the lives of my children. Thank You, Holy Spirit, for Your help and protection. I welcome the peace and love of God into our hearts. Amen (Isa. 54:17; John 10:10).

When the enemy plants seeds of greed and envy

Father, help my children to be conscious that You provide our needs and it's not based on our own efforts or ability. All the earth's resources belong to You. Help my children to feel satisfied and not to be tempted by the love of money or the desire to be rich. I declare that my children will seek the Lord and they will not lack any good thing (Ps. 34:10; Hag. 2:8; 1 Tim. 6:8–10).

When the enemy causes feelings of hopelessness

Lord, thank You for filling my children with hope, joy, and peace, that they may abound in hope by the power of the Holy Spirit (Rom. 15:13).

When the enemy tempts your child with carnal or impure desires

Father, I ask the Holy Spirit to help my children overcome all temptations. Set them free from all learned habits that do not honor You. In the name of Jesus I bring every evil thought that invades their minds into captivity to the obedience of Christ (2 Cor. 10:5; Gal. 5:19–21; Eph. 5:3–7).

Help them, Holy Spirit, to guard their thoughts and desires. "For out of the heart proceed evil thoughts, murders, adulteries, fornications, thefts, false witness, blasphemies. These are the things which defile a man" (Matt. 15:19–20).

When the enemy plants seeds of pride and vanity

Lord, keep my children's hearts from pride and their eyes from haughtiness and arrogance. Help them to base their confidence on their identity in Christ and not on their own looks or abilities. Turn their eyes from looking at worthless and vain things, and revive them in Your way and in Your precepts (Isa. 2:11; 16:6–12; Ezek. 28:17; Ps. 119:37).

Battling the sinful nature

Lord Jesus, thank You for the new nature You have given my children. They are not the same. Thank You for filling their lives with mercy, kindness, humility, gentleness, and patience. Help them not to desire the things of the past but to surrender themselves to You, Lord. Amen (Rom. 6:6; Eph. 4:22–32; Col. 3:1–14).

Resisting lukewarmness

Help my children, Father, to remain firm and to be found faithful, not lukewarm but surrendered completely to the kingdom of God (1 Cor. 4:2; Rev. 3:16).

Overcoming despair and anguish

Father, in this moment of despair and anguish, help my children not to lose courage. Help them to find strength in You and trust You, and in the shadow of Your wings let them take refuge until the storms pass (1 Sam. 30:6; Ps. 57:1).

When the enemy plants seeds of corruption

Father, I thank You because You will not allow my children's lives to end up in the grave, nor will You allow Your faithful servants to suffer corruption (Ps. 16:10).

When your family experiences a death

Thank You, Father, because death is swallowed up in victory through our Lord Jesus Christ, who holds the keys to death and Hades, and my children have the wonderful promise that whoever believes in Him will not perish but have everlasting life (John 3:15; 1 Cor. 15:56–57; Rev. 1:18; 20:14).

Lies of the enemy

Lord, protect my children's minds from believing in the lies of the enemy. Your Word declares that no weapon formed against them shall prosper, and You will condemn every tongue which rises against them in judgment (1 Kings 22:19–23; Isa. 54:17; Rev. 21:8; 22:15).

Attitudes of envy, criticism, and impatience

My Lord, deliver my children's hearts from allowing a bad attitude to invade their lives, making Your blessing depart from them and hindering healing from manifesting promptly. Allow patience to have its perfect work so they may be perfect and complete, lacking nothing (Isa. 58:8–9; Gal. 5:19–21; Eph. 4:31; Col. 3:5–8; Jas. 1:3–4).

Witchcraft and its works

My God, if anything adverse in my children's lives is caused by witchcraft or the occult, either from my own past or inherited from my ancestors, I repent from it now, and I ask You to forgive all my sins and iniquities. I bind every demonic spirit involved, and I order it to come out of my life and the life of my family. I release the healing power of God and decree a complete restoration of all the things that the enemy has stolen from me, in the name of Jesus. Amen (Exod. 22:18; Lev. 19:31; 20:6; Deut. 18:10–12; Nah. 3:4).

False prophecies

Holy Spirit, I ask You to grant my children wisdom and discernment to be able to differentiate between the false prophecies and prophecies that come from the Spirit of God. Teach them to test if the spirits are from God because many false prophets have come into the world (Matt. 7:15–23). As Your Word declares, "Every spirit that confesses that Jesus Christ has come in the flesh is of God, and every spirit that does not confess that Jesus Christ has come in the flesh is not of God. And this is the spirit of the Antichrist, which you have heard was coming, and is now already in the world" (1 John 4:2–3).

Evil or demonic attack

Thank You, Father, that because Jesus defeated the devil on the cross of Calvary, the devil has no part in my children's lives. You are faithful to protect them from the evil one. The devil was cast out from heaven, and You will establish my children and shield them from all evil (Gen. 3:15; Isa. 27:1; 2 Thess. 3:3; Rev. 12:7–9).

Idolatry

Lord, Your command to Your children is clear: "You shall have no other gods before Me. You shall not make for yourself a carved image—any likeness of anything that is in heaven above, or that is in the earth beneath, or that is in the water under the earth; you shall not bow down to them nor serve them. For I, the LORD your God, am a jealous God, visiting the iniquity of the fathers upon the children to the third and fourth generations of those who hate Me" (Exod. 20:3–5).

Father, if my family has transgressed this commandment, help us to discern all the things that could be considered idols and that rob us of our time and our love for You. Thank You, Holy Spirit, for Your help (1 Cor. 10:19–20; Rev. 9:20).

Spirit of error

Father, Your Spirit clearly says that in the latter days some will depart from the faith, listening to deceiving spirits and doctrines of demons. These doctrines emanate from the hypocrisy of liars, whose conscience is seared with the hot iron of their evil deeds. Help my family to discern between the Spirit of truth and the spirit of error (1 Tim. 4:1–2).

Secret agreements with death or the devil

> *Father, if at any moment a secret agreement has been made with death or with the devil against my person or my lineage, I appeal to the blood of Jesus, and I cancel every pact or agreement that may have been made against us, whether in ignorance or intentionally. In the name of Jesus I declare myself and my children free from every curse against us (Isa. 28:17–18).*

Sadness

> *Thank You, my Lord, because You are my children's strength and fortress. You turn their sorrow into joy. You heal their broken spirit. They will not give in to sadness, because the joy of the Lord is their strength. They will maintain a happy heart because it is like good medicine* (Neh. 8:10; Prov. 17:22).

If you follow the teachings and counsel in this book, your life and the lives of your loved ones will change and be transformed. You will protect your heart and the heart of your child. To God be all the glory.

GET TO THE HEART

Use this space to write down the situations in your family that you are praying for and any Scripture verses that the Lord is bringing to your mind as you pray.

_____

_____

_____

Chapter 8

BREAK STRONGHOLDS
IN THE HOME

For though we walk in the flesh, we do not war according to the flesh. For the weapons of our warfare are not carnal but mighty in God for pulling down strongholds, casting down arguments and every high thing that exalts itself against the knowledge of God, bringing every thought into captivity to the obedience of Christ.
—2 CORINTHIANS 10:3–5

TODAY WE HAVE the Spirit of the Lord our healer living in us, restoring and renewing all the things that are out of place, if by faith we believe it. We cannot allow anxiety, depression, disease, and adverse circumstances to steal our joy and our promises of blessing. All adversity must become a springboard that will lead us higher in Christ Jesus.

Earlier I shared powerful prayers to protect and heal your child physically, mentally, and emotionally. If you've prayed these prayers but you've seen no change, don't be discouraged. Continue faithfully in your prayers. However, when a persistent problem in a family continues despite prayers, sometimes a deeper root is involved. This deeper problem is often called a stronghold of the enemy, a generational curse, or a familiar spirit. No matter what you call it, it is a deeply rooted issue that has been in a family for years and continues to repeat itself in a pattern of destruction in generation after generation. It might take more targeted prayers that get to the root of the issue to see your family break free from this type of stronghold.

This chapter will help you learn how to break deeply rooted family patterns that might be the cause of your child's problem. It will also help you understand how to pray for children who are in serious situations, such as rebellion or addiction, and prodigal children who are not living for God.

The Scriptures are active, dynamic, and powerful to destroy and tear down strongholds, curses, and all bad attitudes and behavior. The strongholds from the enemy against you and your children are very real. But the Word tells you that you have powerful weapons. Using the sword of the Spirit (the Word of God) in your mouth, your thoughts, and your heart, you are able to launch your prayers with confidence. That's why I felt it was essential to prepare your heart and mind at the beginning of this book. As you use the Word of God in your mouth, mind, and heart, you are destroying strongholds and disarming evil spirits that are fighting against the lives of your children.

THE IMPORTANCE OF BREAKING THE CYCLE

Jeremiah 32:18 says, "You show lovingkindness to thousands, and repay the iniquity of the fathers into the bosom of their children after them—the Great, the Mighty God, whose name is the LORD of hosts." This verse teaches us a great truth: the sins of the parents are transferred to the children. The Word is clear that God punishes the sins of the parents in their children after them. It is only when a repentant parent stands in the gap for the children and breaks the inherited curses that the children may be free. As long as they are linked to the curse of parents, negative and dysfunctional behavior can continue to occur for many generations.

The parents are the ones who establish roots that will develop the character and behavior of the children. When a parent is willing to change and receive specific prayer to cancel curses, sins, and customs that do not please God, the family will begin to see significant changes in the behavior and atmosphere of the home and personal relationships.

What is true about sin is also true about wounds. When a child is emotionally hurt in his or her family relationships, the child's behavior and character are affected in an adverse and negative way. We need to have a compassionate heart for the injured people we know. But we also have to be careful as parents not to hurt our children and cause negative changes in their character and behavior. It does not mean that we give way to sin but that we are compassionate and help them to heal.

If, as a parent, you still need to heal from the hurts of the past, my wish is that through this book you can find complete healing as you read the advice and prayers. Speak them over yourself as well as your children. If you do not, the curses continue to go from parents to children. It is vital that you break the curses and strongholds of the past in your family. Praying a prayer like this one will greatly impact the deliverance of your family.

> *Holy Spirit, at this moment I need Your wisdom, understanding, and protection to make this powerful prayer.*
>
> *Dear Father, I belong to You, and I want to serve You with all my heart. I surrender to You as I stand in the gap for my family. Forgive me for everything that detains my freedom in Christ Jesus and stops me from enjoying all Your promises. Cleanse my mind and my heart of all the wrong teachings and false doctrines that may have affected my behavior.*
>
> *I ask Your forgiveness for every word I may have spoken in ignorance that has caused any curses over my family and me. Forgive me and deliver me from every evil thought and desire. Sever every relationship and commitment outside of Your will in my life, and forgive every*

perverse and immoral act committed against my body. Break every curse that may have been transferred through the blood of my parents, grandparents, or ancestors; every foul spirit and the spirit of rejection; and all disease and sickness inherited through the blood of my parents, grandparents, and ancestors.

Dear Father, forgive me and deliver me from the curses of poverty, ignorance, shame, and condemnation; from the spirits of death and abortion; from the curses rooted in acts of witchcraft and secret vows in my family and ancestors. In the name of Jesus Christ I rebuke, break, and unbind every curse, spell, and secret covenant, all powers of enchantment and sorcery, and every plan and strategy of Satan against me and my family, from my relatives on both sides of my family and up to ten generations of the past.

I release my children, myself, and my family of all evil spirits connected and related to occult people or practices. I ask You, heavenly Father, to return them from where they were sent and that the curses be upon them.

Today I surrender completely to Your lordship and consecrate myself to serve You and be obedient and devoted to Your Word. Transform my heart and my mind. Help me to be faithful and dedicated to my family and my marital vows. I thank You for this great deliverance in my life and in my family. We are free in the mighty name of Jesus. Amen!

POWERFUL PRAYERS AND DECLARATIONS TO BREAK STRONGHOLDS

It is of great importance that we demonstrate our faith and love for God. Jesus Christ is our Savior, and He heals us of all our sufferings and tribulations. Our children need to see God's love at home without hypocrisy or double-mindedness.

Too many parents are so busy working or involved in social

media that they barely notice who has been feeding the hearts and minds of their children. Think on this before it is too late. Make time for your children. Ask them questions. Admire something in them every day. Learn to stop criticizing, even if you have a great desire to do so.

Declare their identity in Christ Jesus by faith (see chapter 6) and not by what you see in the natural (in their appearance or actions). Declare that they are children of the kingdom of God and that Satan can't have them! The defiant and rebellious child needs love, affection, and powerful prayers. Enter into agreement with the Word of God. Rebuke all doubts, fear, anxiety, and anger. Here are some examples of prayers that will help accomplish these goals.

Rebellion

> *Father God, my children are lost and without Your protection and guidance. Lord, Your promises never change. I rebuke the works of the enemy in my children's lives, and in the name of Jesus I come against all the strongholds of the enemy attacking my family. I come against all evil spirits that keep my children bound, confused, full of unbelief, and unwilling to give their lives to the will of God.*
>
> *Thank You, Lord, for Your promise in Matthew 16:19 that everything we bind on earth will be bound in heaven, and everything we loose (release) on earth will be loosed in heaven. I bind the evil plans of the enemy to interfere in my family and my children's lives. I ask that You give the angels of heaven charge over them, according to Psalm 91. I pray that You release blessings and great favor over my family and cause my children to always walk in Your will for their entire lives.*
>
> *I declare that my children and my family will serve You. Father, I believe that I will stand fast in Your liberty and*

not be entangled with the yoke of bondage, as Galatians 5:1 states. I thank You for setting us free and redeeming us with the blood of Jesus. In the name of Jesus, amen.

Aggression and anger

Lord my God, I need your guidance and wisdom to pray with boldness for my son/daughter to break every yoke of rebellion and disobedience. In the name of Jesus I come against the works of the enemy and the spirit of aggression and anger from invading and influencing his/her life. I bind every plan of the enemy and every satanic assignment to control his/her life. In the name of Jesus I cast out every spirit of the enemy assigned to bring rebellion and hate to my child. In the name of Jesus I release peace and the transforming love of God to enter my child's heart and deliver his/her life from every stronghold of the enemy.

Help me, dear Father, to have patience and be an example of Your love. Open my mouth with wisdom, and close my mouth when I shouldn't speak. Thank You for all Your help and divine guidance. Thank You for the hedge of protection You have around my family. I declare that no attack or weapon formed against my child will triumph. I believe that all my family members are heirs to Your kingdom. In the mighty name of Jesus, amen.

Addiction

I know parents whose sons and daughters have been in and out of rehab and recovery units for years. Yet they are quick to respond to their child's need and will take their child to as many rehab centers as necessary in hopes of a miracle.

An attitude of persistence is essential. Your bulldog determination and powerful prayers may be the only thing your child can depend upon.

Perhaps you have fought with the powers of darkness so long until you are weighed down over the continual struggle. Maybe you have cried so much until you have no more ability to weep. You have been robbed of your joy, and if such a thing as happiness exists, at best it is something from your distant past.

These kinds of battles have a way of changing you while you are in the process of dealing with your rebellious child. Perhaps you don't even recognize yourself and the person you've become. The devil has distorted you, your home life, and relationships. And if anything, it is possible you've grown as mean-spirited as your lost and crazy kids.

You must be persistent to keep a balance in your life and make time for happiness and joy. I understand the pressures and the intense agony of a child in prison, an impending prison sentence, or a child who is in and out of rehab, but life goes on, and so do you. Your other children deserve to have healthy parents, and your spouse needs you as a loving mate.

Do not allow continual conflicts in your home from a rebellious and wayward child. This type of environment ushers in a spirit of bickering, turning your home into a raging inferno of strife. These spirits of conflict will drain you of civility, faith, and happiness.

Tell your kids of your decision, and stand your ground. I have known parents who tolerate the worst kind of behavior from a child thinking that their tolerance will show acceptance.

Life is a journey where unexpected things happen, many of which you cannot control. But you can determine not to allow anything to steal your happiness, kill your joy, or rob you of peace.

God's peace passes all understanding. Allow God's joy to fill your empty heart and life. Use your God-given authority to stop the thunder and lightning brought about by your child's screaming and shouting. Then, allow the Prince of Peace to come into your home and roll the clouds away because this is His specialty.

God does not have bad days. Nor does He ever get too busy to shine the sunlight of His love upon you. He intends to bring joy and gladness into your weary heart.

It took my mother many years of intercession and prayers for two of her teenage sons who had turned their lives to drug addiction. These boys were reared in a divided home with a dad who turned away from God and totally ignored his children. My loving mom never gave up. When things seemed totally impossible, she increased in faith, love, and prayer. Even though my two brothers died too young from the effects of drug addiction, her other seven children were kept by her godly example and powerful prayers. Today some of her grown children are involved in ministry and serving the Lord, and others became professionals and business owners. You must not give up! You must never quit praying specifically and powerfully for them. "For with God nothing [is or ever] shall be impossible" (Luke 1:37, AMP).

Parents, your children are more important than your friends and associates. Invest your love, time, and money in your children. It will be one of the greatest investments you ever make.

Some of you go to bed many nights wondering how you'll be able to face another day of climbing the same mountain you climbed the day before. How long could this thing go on? But remember, the battle will continue until you either win or give up.

You will win significant battles that will turn the tide in your favor. But one battle is not the war, and you must never relinquish the fight until your lost children are safe and secure in the arms of Jesus.

This I do know: once your child has surrendered his or her life to Jesus, the pain and anguish of the battle will be erased by a glorious victory, and therein is the mystery. We never know how close to the final victory we might be, so we can never give up and walk away.

If you are afraid, if you sigh more than you sing, if your heart's desire is to get closer to God, but you feel beaten back in your struggles, the Lord will give you His love, His grace, and His favor. Don't be afraid to believe.

Don't allow Satan to march into your heart, your home, and

your mind to take control. In Jesus' name, stand up and rebuke the forces of hell, and start having yourself a praise party. God is on the throne, and you are His delight.

Start praying some of these powerful prayers with great authority. Take them with you everywhere you go. Make faith declarations. Believe in your heart that your children are free from all bondage and addictions. Allow the Holy Spirit to help you. Never give up!

This counsel for parents with children with addictions was given to me by a very respectable minister of the gospel of more than eighty years of age, who suffered greatly with his daughter addicted to drugs and prostitution, leaving him to care for his two young grandchildren until they became adults. He was able to see God's hand of mercy create miracles and rescue his daughter from hell itself. He did not wish me to give him credit or mention his name, but I know God is allowing your heart to be healed as you read this counsel. Keep interceding and praying for your addicted and wayward children. God is very aware of your prayers, and He will protect the hearts of your children!

Protection from addictive substances

> Lord, I am confident that my children are heirs of the kingdom of God, and I am convinced that my faith-filled prayers have a divine and long-lasting effect on their lives. I ask You to please give them the wisdom to make right decisions in every situation where they have to choose between good and evil. Keep them away from all addictive and harmful substances that may cross their paths. Thank You because the fear of the Lord is their strength. In the name of Jesus, amen.

To resist temptation and peer pressure

Dear God, please help my children to resist temptation to get involved in any kind of substance abuse and drugs used by any of their friends or easily available to them. Rescue them from evil, as You taught us to pray. Help them, dear Holy Spirit, to repel and know in their hearts that any form of addiction will place them in bondage and forfeit God's blessings for their lives. Thank You, Father, for Your hedge of protection around them and for Your angels that protect and keep them from all temptations. In Jesus' name, amen (Luke 11:4; Hos. 2:6; Ps. 91:11–12).

Prayer to break the spirit of addiction

My Lord, I believe Your powerful Word can set my son/ daughter free from all addictions and bondages from the enemy. In the name of Jesus I rebuke the spirits keeping my child bound. I bind the evil spirits of addiction and cast them out right now in the name of Jesus Christ. I release the peace and healing power of God to restore my child. Thank You, my Lord, for bringing my son/daughter to his/her right mind and teaching him/her that he/she can resist the devil. In Jesus' name I believe he/she is free from all addictions and infirmities. Thank You, Holy Spirit, for indwelling my son/daughter and helping him/ her in the process of healing and transformation. In Jesus' name, amen (Jas. 4:7; Ps. 50:15; Phil. 4:13).

PRAYING FOR PRODIGAL CHILDREN

My mother-in-law had four sons and one daughter. My husband, John, is her oldest son. They were all raised in a Christian home, and their father was a prominent pastor in Brooklyn, New York, in one of the largest Hispanic Pentecostal churches in Brooklyn during that time. Their father was always so busy with his congregation that he hardly spent any quality time with his children.

Their mother was a woman of prayer who devoted time to the children and learned to hide the problems that would arise in the school and the home because she knew the scolding and beatings would be dramatic. Three of the sons got involved in drugs in their teens, and two of them died too young.

My husband escaped the drug scene because he was the oldest and had a job from an early age that he really liked. I remember some of the specific prayers this dear mother made for her children. My mother-in-law stood in the gap, continually reminding God and repeating a promise from the Word: "Believe on the Lord Jesus Christ, and you will be saved, *you and your household*" (Acts 16:31, emphasis added).

She prayed for fourteen years, reminding God of His promises that her household (her family) would also be saved, and finally her prodigal sons began to return from the enemy's camp. All of them were saved from eternal damnation, and even though two of them died too young from the effects of the drugs, they died saved.

Today two of them are in successful full-time ministry. One of them pastored a large church for many years, and before retirement he had the honor of passing his baton to his son, who has taken it to the next level with extraordinary success.

For God, all things are possible. Believe God, and you will see the reward. If we want to walk with God, we must agree with Him, saying and believing what His Word says. *With great courage, stand in the gap with your powerful prayers for your children every day!*

This devout mother learned to stand in the gap every day. She made it a habit every morning, just like brushing her teeth. Her dynamic, focused, and full-of-the-Word prayers protected the lives and souls of her children. Nothing is impossible for God, but He needs your faith in action. Declare and believe this prayer:

I declare in faith that my children are heirs to the kingdom of God. Lord, I stand firm on Your promise in Acts 16:31, believing Your Word. I thank You, Father, because I am confident that even if my children pass through the valley of the shadow of death, I will not fear because You are watchful of them to guide their paths. I thank You for this consolation. In the mighty name of Jesus Christ, amen.

Do not become discouraged. You may not always know what is happening in a particular situation, but God is faithful, and you can trust Him. "His mercy is everlasting, and His truth endures to all generations" (Ps. 100:5).

SCRIPTURES TO CLAIM FOR YOUR PRODIGAL CHILDREN

Here are some scriptures you can declare in your own words. They are God's promises for your prodigal children.

And I will establish My covenant between Me and you and your descendants after you in their generations, for an everlasting covenant, to be God to you and your descendants after you.

—GENESIS 17:7

Refrain your voice from weeping, and your eyes from tears; for your work shall be rewarded, says the LORD, and they shall come back from the land of the enemy. There is hope in your future, says the LORD, that your children shall come back to their own border.

—JEREMIAH 31:16–17

Even the captives of the mighty shall be taken away, and the prey of the terrible be delivered; for I will contend with him who contends with you, and I will save your children.

—Isaiah 49:25

All your children shall be taught by the Lord, and great shall be the peace of your children.

—Isaiah 54:13

"As for Me," says the Lord, "this is My covenant with them: My Spirit who is upon you, and My words which I have put in your mouth, shall not depart from your mouth, nor from the mouth of your descendants, nor from the mouth of your descendants' descendants," says the Lord, "from this time and forevermore."

—Isaiah 59:21

Therefore know that the Lord your God, He is God, the faithful God who keeps covenant and mercy for a thousand generations with those who love Him and keep His commandments.

—Deuteronomy 7:9

His descendants will be mighty on earth; the generation of the upright will be blessed.

—Psalm 112:2

"For the promise is to you and to your children, and to all who are afar off, as many as the Lord our God will call." And with many other words he testified and exhorted them, saying, "Be saved from this perverse generation."

—Acts 2:39–40

…that you may become blameless and harmless, children of God without fault in the midst of a crooked and perverse generation, among whom you shine as lights in the world.

—Philippians 2:15

When your child does return to the Lord, here is an example of a prayer you can lead him or her in praying:

Lord Jesus, I need You in my life. I acknowledge that I have sinned and have been disobedient to You and to my parents. I am ready to exchange my life of misery and rebellion for Your gift of salvation. I am willing and ready to trust in You as my Lord and Savior. Thank You, my Lord Jesus, for accepting me as Your son/daughter. I confess and believe that You are the Son of God and You died on the cross and rose again to reign forever. Thank You for cleansing me and forgiving all my sins and giving me the gift of eternal life. Come into my heart, Lord Jesus, as my Lord and Savior. Amen (1 John 1:9; Ps. 51:1).

Always remember this: ignorance will keep a person bound and ignorant. We, as Christians, who have the truth at our disposal, must learn what the Word of God says about us and the provisions already made available for a victorious life. We cannot remain ignorant any longer. We must engage in spiritual warfare and fervent prayers for our loved ones and stop the disintegration of our families. I challenge you to step out of the realm of ignorance and into the wonderful realm of God's wisdom and understanding. "Then you will know the truth, and the truth will set you free" (John 8:32, niv).[1]

Get to the Heart

Use this space to write down the situations in your child's life that you are praying for and any Scripture verses the Lord is bringing to your mind as you pray.

_____

_____

_____

_____

_____

_____

_____

_____

_____

_____

_____

_____

_____

_____

_____

_____

_____

Chapter 9

EFFECTIVE AND POWERFUL SINGLE PARENTING

I will guide you along the best pathway for your
life. I will advise you and watch over you.
—Psalm 32:8, nlt

Years ago my husband and I were the pastors of the single-adult ministry in the church we attended. The group was a mix of those who had never married, divorced singles, and single parents, and they taught us quite a few very important things. The most urgent problems were among the single and divorced parents who were dealing with all the daily parenting issues.

I realize this book is about teaching you how to pray powerful and effective prayers for your children, and later in this chapter I've provided some sample prayers for single-parent households. But it's also urgent to take a critical look at your parenting style and coping skills and the effect they are having on you as the parent and on your child.

Is there peace in your heart and your home? Is your child well-behaved and well-adjusted? Are you receiving spiritual help and encouragement from your local church, and is your child receiving biblical teaching and enjoying fun activities at church?

These are important questions to ponder. Many of you can answer positively, but many more of you are facing great battles, and spiritual nourishment is the last thing on your mind. To heal, you must get into a different environment. Even if disappointments and regrets are clouding your mind daily, you must allow the Holy Spirit, your helper, to begin a healing process in you, or your situation may never change. God did not create you to face life alone (John 14:26).

Allow me to share some of the life-changing counsel we gave to our single and divorced parents and how we saw firsthand many dramatic changes and transformation take place. I pray that you and your child will experience hope and wholeness. The learning, growing, and becoming will be the best parts of your journey.

+ Get connected to a good, vibrant, happy church. This is my first and most important piece of advice. God is able to make all things new (2 Cor. 5:17; Rev. 21:5). Have the pastor and his wife pray you through a prayer of forgiveness and surrender and invoke a blessing over you and your child. Ask them to recommend someone who can become your prayer partner and mentor. You need someone you can lean on and share your burdens with (Gal. 6:2).

+ Pray with your children. Not only pray for them, but teach them how to pray to be forgiven and to forgive others, for their meals, before they head out to school, a bedtime prayer, for healing, for good grades in school, and so on. This will develop faith in your child. "And the prayer of faith will save the sick, and the Lord will raise him up. And if he has committed sins, he will be forgiven" (Jas. 5:15).

+ Be specific and calculated with your instructions and discipline. Let your child know there are consequences for not following instructions and obeying. Don't assume your child will learn everything in school or at day care. Verbalize instructions until he or she gets it. Compliment good behavior, and deal with bad behavior with physical discipline (Prov. 13:24).

+ You will always be the real and most important model of the behavior your child will imitate. Think about this. It's not so much what you say but what you do that will influence his or her life and behavior. Your goal should always be to depend on Christ for everything. As children of God, we must live by faith and not by what we see and know. Allow God Almighty to restore all the brokenness (Gal. 2:20).

+ Develop a royalty mentality. Your heavenly Father is a king! He created *you* and your child as royalty. See yourself crowned and able to enjoy all God's blessings! Spend some time thinking about and studying this. Start acting, thinking, talking, and praying like royalty. It will change your mind-set and desires. Teach your children to do everything like kings' kids with the behavior of royalty! "But you are a chosen generation, a royal priesthood, a holy nation, His own special people, that you may proclaim the praises of Him who called you out of darkness into His marvelous light" (1 Pet. 2:9; see also 1 Sam. 10:25).

+ Stop complaining. Develop a positive and uplifting attitude, and maintain it all the time. It is contagious. Teach your child what the Word says about our words. Practice until you both get it right! It will transform your lives (Prov. 6:2; Matt. 12:37).

+ Be generous with your hugs, kisses, and little surprises and celebrations. Pay attention to your child's emotions and feelings.

+ Be your child's counselor. Protect your child's heart. Get into your child's mind. Find out what makes him or her happy, sad, or ashamed. Teach your child that whatever he or she allows into his or her heart will develop roots and grow and will determine your child's future. That's a big deal! "Keep your heart with all diligence, for out of it spring the issues of life" (Prov. 4:23).

+ Teach your child the truth about sex and immorality. Don't wait until friends tell your child and tempt him or her. Start while your child is still young. Many excellent Christian resources exist on this topic. I encourage you to research this and ask the Holy Spirit to help you (1 Cor. 6:9–10).

+ Help your child develop convictions that will never be compromised. Powerful convictions lead the way to important rules, such as not to lie, steal, cheat, do drugs, be immoral, hate, or compromise. Teach your child to love God with all his or her heart. "Like a muddied fountain and a polluted spring is a righteous man who yields and compromises his integrity before the wicked" (Prov. 25:26, AMP).

+ Address the spirit of anger, for it makes a person act wounded. Have the pastor pray for you and your child if anger has become a serious issue. Don't allow this spirit to steal your joy and well-being (Eph. 4:26).

+ Pay attention to the spirit of depression. Get help immediately, or it can lead to devastating behaviors in you and your child. Depression can cause your spirit to fail and go into a devastating pit (Ps. 143:7–8).

+ Avoid sexual immorality and loneliness, for it can lead you into what you may think is harmless or safe sex. Always be on your guard. Protect your child by protecting yourself from all sin. Don't open the door to the enemy (1 Cor. 6:18).

+ Break the power of generational curses by keeping yourself pure and serving God with all your heart. You will open the door to God's protection and to all His blessings when you refuse to repeat all the sinful things you may have been involved in in the past (Deut. 28:15–28).

+ Keep your faith active with faith declarations from God's Word and a daily devotional. As you read a portion daily, personalize your declaration of faith. Here are some powerful ones that I use:

  ✠ Create in me a pure heart, my Lord, and renew a loyal and committed spirit in me (Ps. 51:10).

  ✠ I have the mind of Christ, and I am able to think with clarity (1 Cor. 2:16).

  ✠ God gives me the strength to do all things (Phil. 4:13).

  ✠ I take all negative thoughts captive and make them obedient to Christ (2 Cor. 10:5).

✝ Thank You, God, because Christ says yes to all of Your promises to me, which is why I can say amen and give You glory (2 Cor. 1:20).

✝ Praise God that I am healed by the wounds of Jesus and the punishment He suffered on my behalf (Isa. 53:5).

✝ The Word of God in me is alive and active, transforming my life and my child's life (Heb. 4:12).

✝ Lord, You are my Rock, my Deliverer, my Refuge, my Strength, and my Salvation. I will not be afraid (Ps. 18:2).

✝ Thank You, Holy Spirit, for capacitating me with wisdom, knowledge, and understanding (Prov. 9:10).

◆ Create a routine for important habits. Meals, homework, bedtime, and hygiene are things that should be scheduled at the same time every day. When your child knows what to expect, following the rules becomes a habit. Additionally a consistent routine will help your child feel more secure and help you feel more organized.

◆ Get a handle on finances. Raising a family on one income or relying on an ex-spouse for child support can be one of the hardest aspects of parenting alone. That's why it's important to take steps to budget your money, learn about long-term investments, plan for college and retirement, and, if possible, enhance your earning power by going back to school or getting additional job training.

+ Be consistent with discipline. If you are divorced or separated, work with your child's other parent to create and observe consistent rules and methods of discipline. There's nothing more stressful than having one parent undermine the other. If your child has other caregivers, talk to them about how you expect your child to be disciplined.

+ Answer questions honestly. Inevitably questions will come up about the changes in your family or about the absence of one parent. Answer your child's questions in an open, honest, and age-appropriate way. Make sure that your child gets the help and support he or she needs to deal with difficult emotions.

+ Treat kids like kids. With the absence of a partner, it's sometimes tempting to rely too heavily on children for comfort, companionship, or sympathy. But children have neither the emotional capacity nor the life experience to act as substitute adult partners. If you find yourself depending on your kids too much or expressing your frustrations to them too often, seek out adult friends and family members, or seek counseling, if necessary.

+ Abolish "guilt" from your vocabulary. It's easy for single parents to feel guilty about the time they don't have or the things they can't do or provide for their children. But for your own sense of well-being, it's better to focus on all the things you do accomplish on a daily basis and on all the things you do provide—and don't forget about all the love, attention, and comfort you're responsible for! (If you ever question your day-to-day achievements, just make a list.) If you're feeling guilty about a divorce or other disruption in your home life, think about joining a support group for other divorced parents. Focus on helping your child (and yourself) get the help needed.

+ Take time for your children. Even though the piles of laundry and dirty dishes may beckon, set aside time each day to enjoy your kids. (After all, isn't that what parenting is all about?) Spend quiet time playing, reading, going for a walk, or simply listening to music together, and most importantly, focus on the love between each other and God and on your relationship as a family.

+ Take time for yourself. Likewise, it's important to schedule time for yourself. Even if it's something as simple as reading a book, taking a warm bath, or having a chat with a friend, setting aside a little personal time will give you a chance to refuel.

+ Stay positive. It's easy to become overwhelmed by all the responsibilities and demands of single parenthood. On top of that, you may be experiencing the pain of divorce or the death of a spouse. Despite all your own feelings, though, it's important to maintain a positive attitude since your children are affected by your moods. The best way to deal with stress is to exercise regularly, maintain a proper diet, get enough rest, and seek balance in your life. If you're feeling sad, it's OK to share some of your sentiments with your children, but let them know that they are not the cause of the problems—and that good times lie ahead for all of you.

ADVICE FOR SINGLE DADS

He is a shield to those who walk uprightly.

—PROVERBS 2:7

Divorce and separation many times cause lots of anger and remorse. In such situations it triggers animosity and hurtful emotions to rise up and cause even more hurt and brokenness to the parent as well as to the child. Instead, a dad should learn to heal with his presence and his faith. This will give the wounded child an example of love on display. Never stop providing and expressing love and hugs. It will save the life of the child and may even restore the broken relationship. Leave a legacy for your child, even if it's impossible to live together. Allow the Lord to help you. Remember, "Keep your heart with all diligence, for out of it spring the issues of life" (Prov. 4:23).

Here's a brief list of a few keys to healthy, effective fatherhood. I encourage you to read and study an expanded list in my book *Satan, You Can't Have My Children*.

+ A good father spends time with his children.

+ Do everything you wish your father would have done with you when you were a child.

+ A good father loves, affirms, and cares for his family.

Single dads, your all-knowing Father wants to reveal to you His divine direction and the critical things you should do in every situation. Psalm 32:8 (quoted at the beginning of this chapter) is a beautiful promise of the Father. The Lord expects you to ask for His divine help, and if you ask in accordance with His will, you can be confident that He hears you and will answer your prayers (1 John 5:14–15).

POWERFUL PRAYERS FOR SINGLE PARENTS

These selected and targeted sample prayers are for your personal preparation and edification. Seriously study them and apply them to your life. They will have a very positive effect on your prayer life, and they will also affect the way you parent your child.

Write some of them on cards, or enter them into your cell phone, and carry them with you in the car and in your bag so you can declare them at any moment. The Word of God is always alive and active and powerful to destroy all strongholds and adversities.

Petition to the Holy Spirit.

Holy Spirit, please teach me how to think, how to speak with wisdom, how to process my thoughts, what to say in public, and what to keep private. Teach me, Holy Spirit, how to redeem my time and not waste it with frivolous thoughts without meaning. Help me to achieve extraordinary, honorable, and important things. Help me to be attentive to my family, never underestimating an urgent cry for help and personal attention. Teach me to discern danger and the attacks of the enemy. Thank You for teaching me and helping me. In Jesus' name, amen.

Cleansing the heart

Beloved Father, purify my heart from everything that hinders my intimate relationship with You. Teach me how to be led by the Holy Spirit and how to listen to His voice during my devotionals. I want to remain free of all bondage and established patterns of thinking that do not allow my spiritual growth. Show me the hidden things that do not please You. I want to serve You in spirit and in truth all the days of my life. I want my children to learn the importance of walking and acting with integrity and loyalty. Thank You, my Lord.

For your child's other parent

Dear Father, I want to have Your love for my child's other parent. Help us to forgive each other for past problems and help each other. Help us to cooperate in raising and training up our children in the fear and love of God. Help us never to pass up an opportunity to love and to bless. I bless the mind and the heart of my child's parent. I bless his/her coming in and going out. Protect his/her life from all danger and plans of the enemy. Direct his/her heart always toward You and Your Word. Thank You, Father, for all Your promises and blessings toward us.

To be an example for my children

Beloved Father, I desire to direct my children to walk in the fear of God. I want to be an example of Your love and compassion. Help me to mature and pay more attention to my words. I desire that my children will always ask me for advice and have trust in me. Open my spiritual eyes to know when the enemy is disturbing and stealing the peace in my home. Teach me, Holy Spirit, how to pray with wisdom and understanding. Fill my mouth with words that are saturated with Your love. In the name of Jesus, amen.

To forgive

Dear Father, help me to forgive. I don't want to be a slave to spirits that orchestrate feelings of rejection and sorrow due to a lack of forgiveness. I also want to stay free to release my family from these evil spirits. In the name of

Jesus, I forgive every person who has offended and hurt me. (Name the people you forgive, and declare that they are no longer in your heart and that you are free from all condemnation.) *I pray this in the powerful name of Jesus Christ. Amen!*

Wisdom to manage the home and finances

Abba Father, I need wisdom and understanding to make smart decisions in my home. Show me through Your Word how to be a man/woman who knows how to handle finances and how to make investments that will produce everything my family needs.

Help in the study of the Word

Holy Spirit, help me to study the Word and retain its teachings. Open my eyes, my heart, my ears, and my mind to receive Your wisdom and understanding when I read and study, because Your words are life and medicine for my whole body and for all of my family. Your Word declares in Proverbs 4:20–22, "My son, give attention to my words; incline your ear to my sayings. Do not let them depart from your eyes; keep them in the midst of your heart; for they are life to those who find them, and health to all their flesh."

Intervention of the Holy Spirit

Lord, I lift up my children, believing that Your Holy Spirit will work in their hearts so they can connect with You in all their decisions. Lord, I desire for my children to have a personal encounter with You so that their lives will be transformed and they will be able to impact others with Your love and Your presence. Holy Spirit, help them to know You personally and to come to You for help, teaching, and friendship. Teach them to know You as their Guide, Teacher, Friend, and Counselor. In the name of the Father, of the Son, and of the Holy Spirit, amen.

Prayer of surrender and discernment

I surrender to You, my Lord and Savior. I desire more than anything to grow and mature in Your Word. I want to be a parent full of Your Spirit, to discern when the enemy is trying to introduce his character and rebellion in my children. I want to pray powerfully according to Your Word, renewing my mind every day and not allowing wondering and evil thoughts to take possession of my mind. I want to be an example my children will be able to emulate as they grow. I want to be a blessing to my children. Help me, Holy Spirit, in this endeavor. I'm ready to join this army of spiritual warriors with Your blessing and support every day. I surrender completely to Your care, protection, and provision. In the name of Jesus Christ, amen!

Personal prayer for parents

I declare, O Lord, that You are the restorer of my life and the One who helps me and guides me in my work. I choose not to agree with the thoughts and feelings that the enemy tries to inject into my mind. I stand firm against the traps of the enemy, and I come into agreement with Your plans for my family and me.

"For I know the thoughts that I think toward you, says the LORD, thoughts of peace and not of evil, to give you a future and a hope" (Jer. 29:11). I thank You, Father, because I have confidence that although my children may

pass through the valley of the shadow of death, I will not
fear because You are watchful of them and guide their
paths. I thank You for this encouragement.

Our children need our constant approval, love, admiration, and
attention to overcome all the attacks of the enemy. During our
single-parent ministry years, my husband and I found that many
single and divorced parents are exhausted from juggling complex
work and childcare schedules or distracted by emotional issues,
and they unknowingly cause their children to suffer a lack of
attention and training when they need it most.

As a single parent it is important to purposefully create time
to interact with each of your children individually and listen to
their stories, complaints, questions, and comments. Give them
praise and show approval when they achieve goals, receive good
grades in school, do their homework, and offer to help around the
house. And don't forget to reprimand them when they fail or are
neglectful.

Approval and admiration instill self-esteem and make a child
feel that his or her help and obedience are significant. The opposite
of these feelings is rejection, which is when the child never receives
admiration or approval for his or her efforts and achievements.

In this case children or adolescents feel isolated, and over time
it is possible that they will show a lack of interest in their studies
and find ways to disobey—all to attract the attention of their parents. This is how many young adults end up failing in everything
they do. Always look for something to admire in your child, even if
you do not feel a natural desire to do so. Eventually you will learn
to see things with the eyes and heart of God.

ADVICE FOR MARRIED PARENTS
WHO ARE THINKING OF DIVORCE

Is your marriage on the edge of divorce? Please read this message
from a desperate wife and mother named Maria.

Iris, I'm having overwhelming thoughts that I do not love my husband. I know that God hates divorce. I know it's wrong. But the feelings are overwhelming. My husband is a good man. He does not deserve this, neither do my two precious sons. They would never understand this because my husband and I never fight.

Communication is part of the problem. I have always repressed my feelings. Now I'm finally learning to express myself and say what I need. I know that feelings are very unpredictable and you cannot trust them. I know that if I yield to them, the enemy will have achieved his plan. I do not want to give in to these feelings, but part of me does want to, just to have some peace. I know that part of this is a spiritual battle.

The problem is that I believe the devil more than I believe God. It is a sad place to be! A few years ago I bought your book *Satan, You Can't Have My Marriage*. I'm about to read it again. I need advice.

My response:

Dear Maria, the fact that you are seeking my help lets me know that God is very interested in you and your family. The enemy is waging a strong war against you. A different spirit has stealthily entered your mind, either by words spoken to you, or by you, or by something that you have allowed to enter your mind.

Please take an inventory of the things that made these feelings begin. If in truth it is a lack of communication, then sit down with your husband and begin to communicate your feelings, without condemning or accusing.

Start doing some of the things I recommend in my book about marriage. These recommendations really work. Ask the Holy Spirit to help you become a loving and caring wife and mother.

Please do not think that I am attacking you, but many times to solve a problem, we have to start with ourselves. Satan wants to destroy your marriage and your children. If you allow it, your second situation could be much worse than the first one. Believe me, Satan does not want to bless you with a better marriage with another husband.

Why does God hate divorce? If you look at the scripture in Malachi 2:16, where God says, "I hate divorce" (AMP), as you continue reading, you will notice that He gives the reason: he who divorces "covers his garment with...violence."

Divorce sheds violence, cruelty, hatred, unforgiveness, suicidal thoughts, nightmares, revenge, disobedience, shame, inferiority, rejection, condemnation, and many, many other negative emotions. All this and even more affects millions of children of divorce, as well as the affected spouse.

I recently entered a foreclosed house for sale. When I entered what was once a child's room, I became distressed when I began to read the sensitive phrases written on all the walls: "You destroyed our lives; you abandoned us; why did you leave? Please come back. What happened to our happy family? I hate you!"

Maria, please do not allow the enemy to blind you. Get help. Find a prayer partner in church to pray with you (a mature servant of God).

Whatever you're doing to instill the desire for divorce, stop doing it! Find ways to change your situation with joy and peace. Involve your children. Plan some fun activities with your husband. Ask God to forgive you and cleanse you of every unclean spirit.

Cover yourself with the blood of Jesus, and ask your husband to pray for you.

Start to admire—it's contagious. Your husband will notice it. Many times a husband who is not very demonstrative and not very communicative may never have had a truly loving situation in the home. God will give you the wisdom you need to help him get closer. But take away the idea of divorce from your mind.

Father God, I pray that You will give Maria and her husband wisdom to see how the enemy seeks to destroy their family. Please give them strength to stand firm and understanding to make wise decisions. Hug them with Your love. Open their spiritual eyes, and bring them closer to each other. In the name of Jesus I rebuke the devil from trying to destroy this home. I release God's blessing in their lives. Thank You, Father God, for Your great mercy toward this family. In the name of Jesus, amen!

If you are reading this testimony, and your marriage is sliding down the wrong path, please take the advice I gave to Maria for yourself personally. Take a personal inventory of your heart and the thoughts that come and go in your mind. Pray a prayer over yourself and your marriage similar to the one I wrote for Maria.

BEWARE OF THE SPIRIT OF LUST

The spirit of lust has invaded our atmosphere like a fierce, unbridled tidal wave. It is hard not to be confronted by this spirit daily, whether on the radio, in the news, in the entertainment industry, at the movies, in the fashion industry, or on pornography sites on the internet—all readily available to everyone from children to the elderly.

We all have to decide, whether married or single. God created us to be worshipers. Everyone adores either the only true living God or other gods. When we worship God every day with our prayers, songs, and faith declarations, we open our hearts to receive peace, healing, and divine direction.

To stop the spirit of lust from invading our souls, we must repair the damaged walls and set up a security system. We must refuse to accept poison in our minds. It will not be enough to read good books, ask for prayer, and do a daily devotional. There must be a genuine commitment to close every door of the heart and every window of the eyes to the things that bring lustful temptation with any person or thing, whether real or imaginary.

Temptation will creep over every person who harbors sin in his or her soul. When the soul is surrendered to Christ and the mind is renewed by the Word, the spirit of temptation will not be a problem. If you need help in this area, do not wait. Do something about it immediately.

I recommend you do the following three things:

1. Repent.

2. Submit to God.

3. Forgive.

I also recommend my books. They are full of experience, good advice, and proven ideas and recommendations that will reinforce your inner man and help your personal life.

GET TO THE HEART

Above all, do not give up. Single parenting is the toughest job on earth, but I receive letters and emails every day giving testimony of God's divine intervention in the lives of many families when the principles from this chapter are applied in faith. Trust that God will also do it for you.

Why did I include this advice in this book about powerful prayers you can pray for your children? Often in a divorce or other type of broken relationship, the children suffer most.

We must get tough and learn to depend on God's help to protect our relationships and our children. Satan is not afraid of you, but you must realize that the power of God is greater than the power of the enemy. You can win this battle!

Use this space to take inventory of your current relationship status and how it might be affecting your child. Write any prayers or Scripture verses the Lord brings to your mind as you pray.

_____

_____

_____

_____

_____

_____

_____

_____

_____

_____

_____

_____

_____

Chapter 10

ESTABLISH A SPIRITUAL
SECURITY SYSTEM IN YOUR HOME

*...not returning evil for evil or reviling for reviling,
but on the contrary blessing, knowing that you were
called to this, that you may inherit a blessing.*
—1 PETER 3:9

THERE'S NO DOUBT we need a spiritual security system in our homes. This chapter discusses the importance of establishing a spiritual security system for your children, but I also refer you to my book *Satan, You Can't Have My Marriage*, where I wrote a chapter about the importance of establishing a spiritual security system for your marriage. When a thief enters a house without a security or surveillance system, he or she is able to steal, kill, and destroy. And we know this is what our spiritual enemy, the devil, is seeking to do as well (John 10:10).

In the spiritual realm we establish a supernatural hedge (border) of angelic protection—a spiritual security system—when Jesus Christ, the solid Rock, is our foundation. We build upon this firm foundation with the Word of God in our hearts and minds and on our lips, establishing supernatural protection from the danger around us and evil assignments against us.

When you honor and bless others, you put yourself in the position to receive the blessings and protection of God. The blessing is an inheritance from God you pass to your children. You bless when you speak words of affirmation. It is essential to protect the heart of your child by blessing your spouse and your children.

WHAT DOES BLESSING MEAN?

The dictionary defines *blessing* as "the act or words of a person who blesses; a special favor, mercy, or benefit: the blessings of liberty; a favor or gift bestowed by God, thereby bringing happiness; the invoking of God's favor upon a person."[1] The opposite is curses and lack. As you can see, the blessing of God brings favor and prosperity. Our blessings also produce favor and break curses. Let us keep blessing our spouse and our children!

As I mentioned in chapter 8, when a parent sins, the children suffer the consequences and many times are at risk of repeating the same offense. This is how many learn to walk in rebellion against God. Bad attitudes and bad examples leave a child exposed, like an easy target to evil spirits. Exodus 20:5 says, "I, the LORD your God, am a jealous God, visiting the iniquity of the fathers upon the children."

There is good news! When parents who fear God and believe the Lord is their Rock, Fortress, and Deliverer decide to stand in the gap with powerful prayers for their children and their family, no devil can stop the blessing and protection of God upon them— or their children and their children's children! It is a tremendous responsibility that demands our commitment and our vigilance. "But from everlasting to everlasting the LORD's love is with those who fear him, and his righteousness with their children's children" (Ps. 103:17, NIV).

The problems we face will either help us grow or dominate us, depending on how we respond and act. God is always operating in our lives, even when we don't realize it or understand it. These are times when we should open our mouths with powerful prayers and declarations of God's Word.

THE IMPORTANCE OF A FATHER'S INFLUENCE AND BLESSING

If you are a father reading this, I'm sure you don't want your son to become a spoiled mama's boy. Teaching him to become a real man of God starts with your influence in the home. A son needs affirmation, hugs, kisses, and positive words—not only from his mother but also from his father. In many cases the son who does not receive affirmation from his father tends to be rebellious and disobedient and never learns to love properly or to give affirmation and love to his wife.

Dad, whether you are a good example or a bad one, you are teaching your son how to treat his mother, his sisters, and his future girlfriend or wife. Children imitate their parents. They don't do what we tell them, but they do what they see us do. What a great responsibility every parent has! Here's a sample prayer to help you grow in this area and become the example of a godly husband and father that your son needs.

> *Dear Father, I need Your wisdom and understanding to raise my son in the fear of God and filled with joy and love for his family. Protect me from passivism and disinterest. Help me to recognize the wiles of the enemy against my family. Open my spiritual eyes to see danger when it enters our home. Protect my son from giving in to temptation and to the influence of ungodly friends. Thank You, Father, for Your divine protection over my family. Help me to be a parent filled with Your love and compassion and always ready to obey Your Word. In the name of Jesus, amen.*

The Importance of a Mother's Attention and Blessing

It is the mother in a Jewish home who prepares the meal on the Sabbath (the day of rest; see Exodus 20). She lights the candles and makes the prayer. She's the one who invites rest into her home.

If you are a mother reading this, I encourage you to be the one who invites the peace of the Holy Spirit into your home and the one who imparts the blessing of God to all the family.

We are constantly in spiritual warfare for our homes. There's an intense crisis in most homes today. The moral values have changed and continue changing drastically. The things that were not permissible yesterday are accepted today.

We need powerful men and women filled with the Holy Spirit who will stand in the gap, in front of the battle for the soul of their spouse and their children.

We need to make an evaluation of the condition of our spiritual life so we can open our mouths with confidence and powerfully resist the enemy and speak blessings and words of wisdom. It will dramatically change the atmosphere in your home.

Find a Quiet Place to Release Your Cares

When you enter into God's presence, you will be able to release your cares and receive healing and restoration for your spirit, soul, and body. Not only that, but you will also find direction, communion, the guidance of the Holy Spirit, understanding and wisdom, provision, forgiveness, and power over all the works of the enemy. Your prayers and your words will become very important. In God's presence is where you release your children and your loved ones and all your burdens. This is faith in action.

The power of death and life are in the tongue. Job 22:28 says,

"You will also declare a thing, and it will be established for you; so light will shine on your ways."

When problems come, instead of stating the problem, we can declare by faith that "all is well." We can go to the secret place of prayer and seek God. We can release the Word of God that we have hidden in our hearts.

> Be anxious for nothing, but in everything by prayer and supplication, with thanksgiving, let your requests be made known to God; and the peace of God, which surpasses all understanding, will guard your hearts and minds through Christ Jesus.
> —PHILIPPIANS 4:6–7

THE POWER OF YOUR WORDS

Our words can either cause healing or cause brokenness. During World War II, Mussolini kept Italy immobilized with the power of his words. Hitler also conquered Austria with the power of his words. He did not engage in the use of bombs or infantry, but only words.

Learn to use words specifically and with purpose. Fill your words with God's power and His Word. They will have a significant effect. All our words must be full of goodness, love, and grace. Good words are "like apples of gold in settings of silver" (Prov. 25:11).

Parents, the home environment is the product of the words we speak. Many children fail because of the effects of negative and destructive words. Many marriages end in divorce from the harmful impact of words that cause a wounded heart.

Words can create miracles and also failures. What you say will locate you, establishing the level where you live your life. You cannot live above your own words. If you declare defeat, anxiety, sickness, or disbelief, you will live at that level. "Whoever guards his mouth and tongue keeps his soul from troubles" (Prov. 21:23).

A negative confession will produce negative results. "You are snared by the words of your mouth; you are taken by the words of your mouth" (Prov. 6:2). Words can produce pain or give strength.

The lives of children are tied to the words of their parents and loved ones. A mother or father can fill the heart of a child to accomplish great things and love God—or can, with words, destroy God's purpose for that child. A wife can introduce blessings or curses in the life of her husband by simply speaking words of wisdom or of defeat.

Devastating words fill the mind with confusion. Never repeat scandalous gossip. Guard your lips with goodness. It is time to defeat the strategies of the enemy in our lives. Here's a powerful prayer you can pray that will start you on a path of speaking blessing and not cursing over your family.

> *Abba Father, Your Word is truth. In the name of Jesus I stand in the gap, believing for divine intervention for my family and my children. Help me to be obedient and to allow the Holy Spirit to teach me every day to establish a spiritual security system of divine protection around my family.*
>
> *Your Word declares that You will contend with those who contend with Your children. Your Word says that we are blessed when we come in and when we go out. Your Word claims that Your angels protect us, watch over us, and help us. Thank You for these promises.*
>
> *I confess that my children are Your disciples and are obedient to Your will, no matter what I see, hear, and know. I stand firm by faith. Your Word declares that even when they become old, they will not turn away from You. I believe this promise with all my heart.*
>
> *Father, work in their lives a healthy fear and reverence of You. Help them not only to follow requirements*

and commandments but also to have a passion for the things of You. Move in their lives every day, and help them to put You first in all things and to develop an intimate relationship with the Holy Spirit. Reveal Yourself to them in visions and dreams, in such a way that the revelation of the kingdom of God will always be present in their minds.

I believe my children will know the truth in their hearts and not only in their heads. I believe they will always base their lives on the truth, not on Satan's lies. I believe they will learn every day to renew their minds with the Word of God and to renew their thoughts with all that is pure, noble, true, admirable, excellent, and worthy of praise (John 8:32; Rom. 12:2; Phil. 4:8).

I ask that the joy of the Lord will always be their strength. Fill them with Your joy so they will never be tempted to seek the fleeting pleasures of the world. Help them to discern the tactics of the enemy and not entertain his lies in their minds or be enslaved by his strategies (2 Cor. 2:11; Jas. 4:7). Help them to value Your love and affection more than all the other things in the world.

Father, I surrender my children to Your care, and I have confidence that they will always be blessed by Your faithfulness and great love toward them. I pray that love and truth never depart from my children and that these attributes will be engrained in their hearts, that they may obtain esteem and favor with You and with all people. In the name of Jesus, amen.

Do not give up! Cast out all fear from your heart. Apply the protection Jesus Christ purchased for you with His shed blood on the cross, and arm yourself with the armor of Jesus Christ and the Word of God. Don't give up because you do not see changes quickly. Have patience and wait, even if it takes days, weeks, months, or years. The most important thing is that in the end they will inherit eternal life and salvation.

Now, rejoice with thankfulness. Rebuke the enemy and his foul spirits, and they will flee from you. Apply the blood of Jesus over your body, your family, and your home. God is ready to bless you. Determine with all your heart to establish a spiritual security system in your home.

STOP THE DEVIL FROM ENTERING YOUR HOME!

We defeat the devil through the blood of Jesus and our confession. Declare the Word in faith over your family, and do not allow entry to the enemy in the lives of your children and your marriage. We were created to overcome and to possess God's blessings. The power of God in a child of God is stronger than the power of the enemy!

God did not create you to be ordinary, but to be extraordinary. You were purposefully designed for the miraculous and the supernatural. You must accept and believe in the process that God created to launch you toward these blessings. Here is a sample prayer to build up your faith during this spiritual process.

> *Father God, I will stand firm upon Your immutable Word and Your promises for me. I refuse to be moved by what I feel, see, and know. My position in Christ is secure. No devil in hell can change or alter Your promises for my family and me.*
>
> *I free myself from all predicaments, obstacles, curses, spirits of infirmity, lack, and weakness, and I declare healing and restoration of all things broken in the mighty name of Jesus Christ. Thank you, Abba Father, for helping me remain courageous and secure in my position in Christ Jesus.*

The power of the presence of God will set you free of all strongholds of the enemy. Do not fear. Open your mouth with boldness and declare victory in the name of Jesus. Jeremiah 5:14 says that God can make His words like a fire in your mouth, destroying all diabolical roots. Praise God!

The next step is to start to put the Word of God into action!

TEN ACTIONS THAT STOP THE ENEMY AND ESTABLISH THE BLESSINGS OF GOD IN OUR HOMES

1. Develop a personal friendship with the Holy Spirit.

Speak to Him like a friend. Ask Him sincerely to help you. Ask Him to teach you how to pray and understand the Bible every time you read and study.

2. Make a habit of praying.

Do it every morning and confess victory, protection, healing, and divine intervention in every area of your life.

3. Rebuke the enemy.

Learn to rebuke the enemy every time you feel stressed or fearful, and the enemy has to flee from you.

4. Plead the blood of Jesus.

Jesus' shed blood provides protection over your mind, your body, your spouse, and each member of your family. This is extremely effective. Make it a habit.

5. Stop all negative words, thoughts, complaining, and gossip.

This is extremely important. Every time you allow these words into your home, the enemy will attack you with something because you're giving him permission.

6. Make a habit of going to church.

Attend regularly, and take your children to classes of their age group. Encourage them to get involved in weekly activities at your church.

7. Block all violent and sexual content from movies, games, videos, and TV.

This is an area being overlooked by today's younger parents, and it is an area Satan uses to blind the minds of our children.

8. Read the Bible.

Do a daily devotional, even if it's a short one. If possible, attend discipleship classes. It will help you to bring all negative thoughts captive to the obedience of God.

9. Feed your mind with positive and life-changing books, music, and teachings.

Keep some soft Christian music going all the time. This will help you cast out fear and become peaceful and positive in all you do.

10. Display acts of love between family members and spouses.

Don't hold back on hugs, kisses, blessings, prayers, smiles, and compliments. Eat together as a family, and enjoy conversations. Learn to say, "I love you," "You look good," "I bless you," and other important, affirming statements.

As I close this final chapter, let's review the steps to establish a spiritual security system in your home.

- Make powerful prayers.
- Develop spiritual vigilance.
- Model personal discipline.
- Speak words that edify.

+ Do not speak negative words.

+ Bless all the time.

+ Bind and loose demons.

+ Love and respect your spouse.

+ Pay attention to the needs and changes in attitude.

+ Ask for help from the Holy Spirit and God's angels.

+ Pray in the language of the Holy Spirit.

+ Pray together.

+ Eat together.

+ Play together.

+ Maintain order in all things.

+ Pay attention to your thoughts.

+ Bless: "I bless you. I bless your coming in and going out…"

YOU CAN BEGIN TODAY!

The task and responsibility of establishing a spiritual security system are not complicated, but establishing one does demand attention and care. You will know that you are making progress when it becomes a habit just like preparing a cup of coffee every morning and making sure the doors are locked before going to sleep at night.

Believe and call things that are not as if they are already manifested, without any doubt in your heart. The authority that God has delegated to you is a powerful weapon that you must use on a daily basis (Mark 11:23; Luke 10:19). Your faith will give certainty and confidence to your hope and your prayers based on the Word (Heb. 11:1).

An immense joy awaits you, though you may have to withstand many trials for a time (1 Pet. 1:6). Make a valuable decision to cast out all fear from your heart. You can choose to make a difference in your child's life, no matter what his or her age or circumstance, starting today!

Appendix A

GOD'S PROMISES FOR
ALL CHILDREN

G IVE YOUR FAITH a voice of praise. Make the following declarations of faith based on the Word of God with boldness over your children and family (Ps. 112:1–2).

I confess God's Word over my children, and I declare that they will be filled with faith and a great and sincere love to serve God with all their heart. I believe and confess that my children are heirs to the kingdom of God, obedient to His will (Heb. 10:38; Gal. 3:29; 1 Pet. 1:2).

I decree that my children are in God's hands and that no weapon formed against them will prosper. I am convinced that God's love and protection guard and keep them from all the enemy's attacks and strategies (Isa. 54:17; Phil. 4:7).

I claim that my children are chosen and taught by the Lord and their peace will be great (Isa. 54:13).

I believe and confess that God's warrior angels will protect and defend my children. God is their refuge and their strength (Ps. 91:11–12; 2 Sam. 22:3).

My children will learn to be loyal, of excellent character, loving, patient, generous, and kind, and they will live under the authority of the Holy Spirit (Dan. 6:3; Jas. 5:8; John 14:26).

I declare blessing upon my children. I bind every spirit of the enemy from invading their lives, and I give thanks for the favor and wisdom of God upon their lives (Matt. 16:19; Acts 7:9–10).

I believe that the fear of the Lord is in them to hate evil and that God will guard their souls and deliver them from the hands of the wicked (Ps. 97:10).

My children's hearts will be kept from being rebellious and prideful, and they will be saved from harm (Isa. 50:5; Ps. 106:10).

My children will depart from the ways of sinners, and God will protect them from everyone who tries to deceive them and lead them astray. He will protect them from ungodly relationships and friends (Prov. 1:10–15).

The Holy Spirit will always be active in the hearts of my children, helping them to be responsible in all relationships and also to submit to the authority over them. He will place in them a spirit of excellence, as in the heart of Daniel (Dan. 6:3).

My children can learn not to be afraid and to resist every evil spirit because God's Word declares, "Resist the devil and he will flee from you" (Jas. 4:7).

The Lord will place a hedge of protection around my children, protecting them from all evil and danger (Job 1:10).

My God has warrior angels caring for and guarding the paths of my children (Ps. 91:11).

God's Word declares in Psalm 91 that angels will hold my children up in their hands so that no harm will come to them.

I decree that just as Jesus grew "strong in spirit, filled with wisdom; and the grace of God was upon Him," my children will also grow in wisdom and be strong in spirit and full of grace to be examples to all who know them (Luke 2:40).

My children are protected from all plagues and destruction and from all the traps and snares of the enemy. Thank You, Father, for Your angels that protect and keep them (Ps. 91:11–12).

My children will always have the desire in their hearts to keep and respect all God's commandments (Prov. 3:1).

Godly wisdom will help my children form a lifestyle where generosity, offerings, tithes, and helping the poor become a habit, for in this is an excellent reward and recompense. My children will be cheerful givers, always full of Your blessing and abundance (Prov. 3:9).

I declare that God is a shield, a refuge, and a solid rock and that His right hand always guides, protects, and leads my children (Ps. 144:2; 18:35; 73:23).

God's mercy is eternal and protects my children as they fear Him (Jude 21).

I firmly believe that my children will be restored and God's Word will be fulfilled in their lives. I believe that the lost years will be restituted and their joy shall be great. I give God endless thanks for this promise (Joel 2:25).

I declare that the Almighty will save my children from the hand of the enemy (Isa. 49:25). My children will return to the heart of God.

I believe that my children will keep God's commandments and will persevere in the midst of change and peer pressure (Rev. 3:10).

Satan must remove his hands from my children! I apply the protection that comes from the blood of Jesus Christ over their lives, and I declare that I have authority over all the power of the enemy to stand in the gap for them (1 John 1:7; Luke 10:19).

My fervent prayers for my children produce lasting results (Jas. 5:16). I thank God for this promise.

God hears and is attentive to my cry. "I will cry out to God Most High, to God who performs all things for me" (Ps. 57:2).

I believe and stand steadfast upon God's promise that my children will return from the land of the enemy (Jer. 31:16).

I declare that the covenant of the Lord and the prophetic word in Isaiah 59:21 is also for my children: "This is My covenant with them: My Spirit who is upon you, and My words which I have put in your mouth, shall not depart from your mouth, nor from the mouth of your descendants, nor from the mouth of your descendants' descendants," says the LORD, "from this time and forevermore." Amen!

Appendix B

TEACH YOUR CHILDREN TO PRAY

PARENTS TRAIN THEIR children to do many tasks—from how to dress and coordinate their clothing to how to handle money. I believe the best skill we can teach them is how to follow God's direction. Our almighty Father wants to reveal to us exactly what we should do in every situation. The Lord says: "I will instruct you and teach you in the way you should go; I will guide you with My eye" (Ps. 32:8).

THE MOST IMPORTANT PRAYER!

Direct your children to pray the following prayer no matter their age. The younger, the better. It is also good for them to repeat this prayer when they are older to refresh their minds of the very important meaning of salvation.

The Bible says that "if you confess with your mouth the Lord Jesus and believe in your heart that God has raised Him from the dead, you will be saved. For with the heart one believes unto righteousness, and with the mouth confession is made unto salvation" (Rom. 10:9–10). To receive Jesus Christ as Lord and Savior, please pray this prayer or a similar prayer in your own words. The specific words are not important, but your children must believe with all their hearts what their mouths confess.

Lord Jesus, I want to know You personally. Thank You for dying on the cross for me to pay the price for my sins. I open the door of my life and my heart, and I receive You as my Lord and Savior. Thank You for forgiving all my sins and giving me eternal life. Please take control of my life and help me to overcome and change everything that is out of order and that does not please You. In the name of Jesus, amen.

NOTES

CHAPTER 3

1.   Merriam-Webster, s.v. "discern," accessed January 10, 2019, https://www.merriam-webster.com/dictionary/discern.

2.   Merriam-Webster, s.v. "change," accessed January 10, 2019, https://www.merriam-webster.com/dictionary/change.

CHAPTER 6

1.   "Father Absence and Involvement Statistics," National Fatherhood Initiative, accessed January 10, 2019, https://www.fatherhood.org/fatherhood-data-statistics.

2.   "Common Mental Health Disorders in Young Adults," Foundations Recovery Network, accessed January 10, 2019, https://www.dualdiagnosis.org/mental-health-and-addiction/common-young-adults/.

3.   "Mental Illness in Children," WebMD, accessed January 10, 2019, https://www.webmd.com/mental-health/mental-illness-children#1.

4.   "Mental Illness in Children," WebMD.

CHAPTER 8

1.   Iris Delgado, *Satan, You Can't Have My Children* (Lake Mary, FL: Charisma House, 2011), 91.

CHAPTER 10

1.   Dictionary.com, s.v. "blessing," accessed January 10, 2019, https://www.dictionary.com/browse/blessing.

My FREE GIFT to You:

Be a Prayer Warrior for Your Children.
As My Way of Saying Thank You...

I'm so happy you read my book. It's important to pray a protection over your children, especially in today's world.

I encourage you to explore beyond what is presented in this book. So, as both a thank you and a means to learn more, I am offering you a few gifts:

OVER $50 VALUE

To get these **FREE GIFTS,** please go to:
www.IrisDelgadoBooks.com/gift

Thanks again, and God bless you,

Iris Delgado